AMERICAN DREAM AGAIN

THE STORY OF HOW ONE COMPANY IS HELPING
AMERICANS ELIMINATE DEBT, BUILD REAL
WEALTH, & LIVE THE AMERICAN DREAM AGAIN

DAVID ADLARD

American Dream Again

No claim to copyright is made for original U.S. Government Works.

Disclaimer: This body of work represents the thoughts and words of the author and is not endorsed by Tranont, Tranont Life, NPR, or any of the affiliated companies mentioned in this work.

Tranont Life products are only available from fully licensed representatives.

Every effort has been made to accurately represent the company and the potential of the products.

There is no guarantee that you will earn any money using the techniques and ideas in these materials. Examples in these materials are not to be interpreted as a promise or guarantee of earnings. Earning potential is entirely dependent on the person using these products, ideas and techniques. The author and affiliates do not position this product as a "get rich scheme."

Your level of success in attaining the results referenced in this work depends on the time you devote to the program, ideas and techniques mentioned, your finances, knowledge and various skills. Since these factors differ according to individuals, the author cannot guarantee your success or income level. Nor is the author responsible for any of your actions.

Materials in this work or any related websites may contain information that includes or is based upon forward-looking statements within the meaning of the securities litigation reform act of 1995. Forward-looking statements give our expectations or forecasts of future events. You can identify these statements by the fact that they do not relate strictly to historical or current facts. They use words such as "anticipate," "estimate," "expect," "project," "intend," "plan," "believe," and other words and terms of similar meaning in connection with a description of potential earnings or financial performance.

Any and all forward looking statements here or on any of our sales material are intended to express our opinion of earnings potential. Many factors will be important in determining your actual results and no guarantees are made that you will achieve results similar to ours or anybody else's, in fact no guarantees are made that you will achieve any results from the ideas and techniques in this work material.

This book is dedicated to the brave men and women of our armed services, both past and present. If not for you, living the great American Dream of Entrepreneurship would not be possible. Thank you for providing the freedom we enjoy to pursue our dreams.

TABLE OF CONTENTS

INTRODUCTION

There was once a dream that was America. In the dream, everyone, no matter where they came from, held within them the potential to rise from the lowliest to the loftiest of positions. Do you remember being told as a child that you could do anything you wanted, *be* anything you wanted, even become President of the United States of America? If you were told this, as a child or even later on in life, you are like so many other citizens of this great country.

This dream has animated the imaginations of countless Americans, and immigrants, for decades. In the last century, our nation rose from the ranks of the powers of the western world. We became a leader, standing on the shoulders of giants. Through two world wars, the Cold War and countless imperial and financial entanglements, America has survived and thrived. And common sense shows that this success was built by the back-breaking labor of the American worker.

THE PENSION OF THE GOOD OLD DAYS

In the proverbial "good old days" many of us keep hearing about, the days of your parents and grandparents, you could expect a reward for a few dozen years of hard work. The vision that was instilled into the bones of this country was one of white picket fences, two-car garages and swimming pools in the back yard. And what was the ultimate end of years of service to the local plant, or the U.S. Post Office, or wherever you might have "clocked in" on a daily basis for years upon years on end? The *pension*.

In other words, work hard now so that, when you're old and gray, you won't have to work your fingers to the bone or grind your nose to a nub on the millstone of employment until the day you finally kick the bucket. The essential foundation of an employee pension scheme is the idea that you deserve something at the end of your long labors. A return to your investment, you might say.

HERE'S THE CATCH

You may have noticed, however, that something has gone terribly wrong. High unemployment rates exist right alongside utter job dissatisfaction. Many Americans enjoy a higher standard of living than any previous generation (not to mention the vast majority of the human race), but remain *cash poor*. Earning a lot of money is no guarantee that you will not have to work until the moment your heart gives out. The pensions of yesteryear are all but gone. At the very least, you will not be able to count on one to support yourself (let alone a family) in your retirement.

Fair or unfair, the most important thing to realize is that there is a problem here. Millions upon millions of Americans are currently facing steep uphill battles, working at jobs they can't stand, for a pay rate that leaves something to be desired, to put it politely. This is a calamity that affects the vast majority of the country on every level, emotionally, spiritually and mentally.

WHAT HAPPENED?

I would not presume to speak for you, but this is hardly the America I recognize, the one in which I grew up. So many families are crippled by skyrocketing debt incurred through frivolous spending or a lack of financial literacy (or both!). There is an army of reasons why the America dream has gone south. If you listen closely, you can hear its soldiers stamping their feet and muttering invective. They are just outside your window.

Taxes, mortgages, car payments, tennis lessons for the kids, clothes for the kids, more car payments, a new, bigger house because the baby's on the way, a bigger mortgage, leveraging the credit cards to pay for private schools or piano lessons, college educations for your children… It seems almost as if you must be held locked in a cycle of spending from the moment you set foot in your office, or other place of employment, until the day you leave for the last time. Even at the end of that long road, in today's economic climate, you can't be assured that your pension or your Social Security benefits will survive long enough for you to be able to claim them. Unlike the benefits you expect, however, your liabilities will always stay chained to your ankle, weighing you down.

> ## "Building a better you is the first step in building a better America."
>
> *- Zig Ziglar*

WAIT! THERE IS HOPE

That last paragraph reads as doom and gloom, I know. In order to wake up, though, you have to hear the boom of a thunderclap. You may feel that you have been kneecapped, that you can't hobble away from the wreckage of credit card debt and that second mortgage. You may be shaking your fists at the heavens, shouting, "But I did everything right!"

Still, even in the darkest of nights, there is light to be found. Finding your way out of the wild woods of financial instability and into the open fields of true security, in which you and only you are in control of your destiny, is both a worthwhile pursuit and completely achievable.

Raging, "But I did everything right," is but the beginning. From here on out, we will be looking at the tools you need to become truly financially successful. Done right, this process can show you the path toward earning a higher income than you ever dreamed possible.

"Don't concern yourself too much with how you are going to achieve your goal. Leave that completely to a power greater than yourself. All you have to do is know where you're going. The answers will come to you of their own accord and at the right time."

- Earl Nightingale

USE THAT RIGHTEOUS INDIGNATION TO YOUR ADVANTAGE

Righteous indignation is the first step on the road to fulfilling your goals and living the dream you have always wanted for your life and the life of your family. To combat injustice, it must first be recognized as such. You won't be able to spar with ghosts, so once you arrive at that critical moment when you identify the problem, you will be that much closer to its resolution.

Though there is a long road ahead of you, you have already displayed far more initiative than the better part of American society today. You have almost certainly heard the term "the Rat Race" before. Well, it is very real, as I'm sure you know by now. You are probably caught in it yourself, which is why you turned to this book for guidance.

TOGETHER, WE CAN AND WE WILL FIND A WAY OUT OF THE RAT RACE

Most Americans are so focused on the pursuit of the small scrap of cheese that they are blinded to the walls of the maze.

That sounds thoughtful, you think to yourself, but what does that even mean? Simply put, this bleak little metaphor is meant to illustrate the average American's seemingly chemical addiction to money.

Money, contrary to popular belief, isn't real. More specifically, money is only as real as you believe it to be. It is all a question of how you think about money.

There are two ways in which to regard money. One is healthy, the other not so much.

UNHEALTHY

The unhealthy way is also, unfortunately, the traditional way, that way of thinking inspired by the American dream. Following the first path, you will be told again and again that you should find a "steady job," put money away in your bank account, build up your pension and be content to earn a "a day's pay for a day's work."

There is nothing evil about this at all. In fact, many of those who adhere to these strictures are hard working, honest individuals. Sadly, though, they will never achieve their true potential. They will always find themselves living for work, rather than working to live.

HEALTHY

In stark contrast with the unhealthy way to think about money, the healthy one, the one that leads to true financial independence, is a lot easier to bring about than people realize. The difference is that coming to grips with the system, which is hardly common practice, requires a few mental revolutions (and I meant that in both senses of the word "revolution").

First, you will need to accept that you have to power to change your circumstances. Yes, you can completely revolutionize the way you think about and interact with money. In so doing, you will change the delivery system by which money comes to you, while also, importantly, increasing the volume of the stream.

Second, read through, parse, dissect and absorb the content of this book. The tools, strategies and modes of thinking presented herein will serve as the keystones to the bridge you will be building, a bridge to a resplendently bright tomorrow.

Third, and finally, you will go out into that wide world and apply the lessons you took in as you read. You will never have to succumb to the fear of being financially trapped or helpless ever again. You will be free to pursue your happiness in the manner in which you see fit!

> **"People are always blaming their circumstances for what they are. I don't believe in circumstances. The people who get on in this world are the people who get up and look for the circumstances they want, and if they can't find them, make them."**
>
> - *George Bernard Shaw*

Yes! You can make money that truly belongs to you! And, yes, your money can be made to work for *you*, and this book will show you how to achieve exactly that wonderful state of being.

You can eliminate your debt.

You can build real wealth.

You can live the American dream again.

And you will, so long as you remember:

THE SECRET IS TO CHANGE YOUR MODE OF OPERATIONS

Once we have discussed the old American dream and contrasted it with the New American Dream (chapters 1 and 2, respectively), in chapter 3, we will delve into the nature and activities of a company that is working to empower Americans to break the chains that bind them to their anchoring liabilities, to seize hold of their financial destinies: Tranont, Inc.

BUT LET'S NOT GET AHEAD OF OURSELVES HERE

In chapter 3, we will talk about Tranont, and the tremendous value they bring to the challenge of revitalizing the American dream of starting a small business and growing with it as you grow your personal assets. Before we can do that, though, we will need to fully establish the parameters of the problem we are facing.

You have in all likelihood heard the adage "No use crying over spilt milk." Of course, I agree with this little bit of everyday wisdom, as would just about anybody. However, in an effort to illustrate my point and the greater point of this book, allow me to complicate that statement slightly:

"There is no use in crying over spilt milk. But it would be a good idea to figure out how much milk was spilled, as well as by what means or why it was spilled."

Though we are not being as productive as we might be when we obsess and agonize over the past, we should understand what happened, and why it happened, so that we might learn from our mistakes.

This step is one that will probably lead you (if it has not already done so) to ask, "What happened to America, then?"

With how fast today's world moves, it should not prove too great a surprise that the old way of living the American dream is now impossible. Just as an individual can earn a high salary while remaining cash poor, he can be information rich but deficient in knowledge.

Consider how much raw data is available through the World Wide Web. Collectively, as a society, we have access to a quantity of information unparalleled in the history of the human race. But has that really helped us? Let me rephrase the question: has having access to a wealth of information made you wealthy?

If you are reading this book, I will assume the answer is "no." But that is perfectly alright. In fact, you should revel in the position you find yourself in, at this very instant in time. You are at a crossroads and, with a little whisper in your ear, you can take the path you have always wanted to take, but felt you couldn't afford to the last time you passed on the chance to better your life for good.

A QUESTION FOR THE AGES

Let's boldly ask the question: what was the American Dream?

It may sting a little to admit that the old way is dead, or well on its way to death, but I could not have found the way forward had I not done so. And that same logic applies to anyone in the same boat (all of us!). Admitting there is a problem is necessarily the first step toward committing to solving it.

If you do not agree already — though, if you are reading this book, you may well have worked it out on your own — chapter one will show us what the Old American Dream was, as well as the forces that caused its demise.

Once we have seen, with our own eyes, the nature of the great question hovering in the back of our minds, we will move on to talking about the New American Dream in Chapter 2.

So, what was the American Dream?

There, it's been asked, clearly and concisely. Only now can we hope to begin to find the answer.

I.

That Picket Fence Could Use a Fresh Coat: The Millennial Herd and the Death of the Old American Dream

For folks who grew up in my generation, the mindset that dominated their actions in life was this: go to school, get good grades, earn that college degree, get a job and work 30-40 years at that job. During this last period, you were supposed to get married and buy a house in the suburbs with a black mail box and white picket fence. Throw in a couple of kids and a dog, and you have yourself the idyllic American portrait. In other words, this is what the American Dream looked like to so many of us.

Some still cling to this outdated notion, believing it to be a formula with not one but two answers. Plug in the right variables, do the math and, *pow!*, you have the perfect method for achieving happiness and financial stability.

The trouble is, it doesn't work that way anymore. There are many problems with the above "formula". So many, actually, that we are not blessed with the time to get into them now. We need to cover a lot of bases. As stated above, we can't solve the problem until we have identified its causes. That is why, before I start throwing terms and concepts at you, we are going to look at the American Dream turned American Nightmare.

THE AMERICAN NIGHTMARE

"Get a degree, get a job, work hard, retire on a pension…" That plan might have worked for several generations of Americans, but this age has a pace all its own. Gone are the days in which you could reasonably be expected to find, hold and stay with a job for three decades or more. By that same token, then, dead and gone are the days when you could expect traditional pension schemes to carry you into and through your retirement years.

According to an article published on Forbes.com, the length of time in which today's average worker remains with a single employer is 4.4 years. The "youngest" members of the workforce are foreseen to stick with a particular job for about half that time. These figures come to us from the Bureau of Labor Statistics.

That same article relates another very revealing statistic from the Future Workplace: some ninety-one percent of the Millennial Generation "expect to stay in a job for less than three years." For those of you keeping score at home, the typical Millennial (anyone born between the late seventies or early eighties to the late nineties) will hold well over a *dozen* jobs before he or she retires.

How obvious is it now that the Old Dream is dead?

Those whom Forbes calls "chronic job-hoppers" have changed and will continue to drastically alter the job marketplace. But it is important to remember that the world at large is changing around them, as well. "Job-hopping" is a symptom of a greater disease. To be sure, we are all affected individually to the extent that we participate in this overarching *group-think*.

The Herd Mentality

In America, we value *individualism*. We want you, the individual, to be all you can be. This entails working, starting a family, buying a home and, generally, contributing to the betterment of society. And you are always expected to do so in your own, unique way and by your means.

We know, however, that the "herd mentality" is prevalent here, too. We live in a democracy. In a democracy, by definition, the behavior of the majority is the deciding factor in how life and business are shaped going forward. I have just laid out the bare bones for your consideration. Remember, we are dealing with definitions and logic here, plain and simple.

Now, let me submit another idea for you to think about. It is obviously true that a successful business is one which sells its products or services effectively, is it not? Therefore, the *most* successful business is the one which generates the most dollars from custom. This does not necessarily mean that a business needs to sell *more*. For example, a shoe store that sells more plastic sandals may not end up making more money than the store that sells leather dress shoes. Still, whichever of the two hypothetical shoe stores named above moves its product the most effectively wins out in the end. A better bottom line is the winner's ultimate reward.

But what is the difference between a successful shoe store and a less successful one? The answer is so simple that it's staring you right in the face. It is one of those answers you knew, and you knew that you knew it, like the one you couldn't get out before someone beat you to it that one day during a lecture on semi-permeable membranes in college.

The answer is this: a winning product is one that people want to buy. Scratch that — they feel they *need* to buy it or they will be missing out, somehow. Do they *really* need it? It doesn't matter, actually. The better shoe store's marketing efforts convinced the consumer. This store gave the people what they wanted by convincing them that they wanted it in the first place.

Why am I going on and on about shoe marketing and consumers? Well, this little thought experiment should serve as stand-in for the state of America today.

TOO MANY PEOPLE BLEAT THEMSELVES DRY

Consumerism has been both boon and bane to our society, but in very different ways. A boon in that our economy rose the very top in the world; a bane in what it has meant for the wallets and pocketbooks of Americans all across the country.

I have heard it said that we vote with our wallets. That much seems self-evident to me. In America, our "one-man, one-vote" system of capitalism has produced some of the finest technologies and works of genius the world has ever seen. In addition, our industry, work ethic and ingenuity drove us to the top of the world' economic ladder.

There was, however, a downside to this tremendous boost in affluence. With great material wealth came a shift in consciousness. It is hard to say when exactly it began, but it is more important to know that we are in the grips of this creature even now.

The impact of the latest herd of bleating sheep, the Millennial Herd, promises to continue and worsen the worrying trends which have grown dominant over the past few decades.

Bullet points will not make these issues any less daunting, but maybe they will be more easily digestible:

- Record college costs with no guarantee of a job at the end of the four, five, six years that the average student will spend earning a Bachelor's (Science or Art)
- Student loans crippling individuals and couples just starting out
- The outlook for Master's Degrees isn't much sunnier
- Forget about the outrageous costs involved in earning a degree in medicine or law
- Rampant credit card debt
- Massive foreclosure rates
- An emphasis on maintaining an unrealistic lifestyle, taking out a second mortgage to manage it
- Working well past retirement age, into one's seventies (and beyond)

This list is in no way comprehensive because it does not intend to be. These are but a few of the problems facing the American workers, entrepreneurs, businesspeople and investors of the twenty-first century. That is why we are going to perform a brief rundown of each of these, to relate just how necessary it is to be mindful going forward.

You want to be free of the concerns listed above, which is why you need to understand the scope of these damaging attributes of society. Again, the only way you can free yourself is to know the path that lies before you and what separates it from the others you might take. Be aware that there will be many pitfalls along the way, but the advice given in this book is meant to see you through many a hardship.

You are different from the sheep, because you are actively seeking to better and, eventually, perfect your financial situation. Let's examine what lies in store for the sheep, those consumers who are content to bleat themselves dry of every potential revenue stream they might have harnessed. That way you can be sure to sidestep any pitfall you might come across.

CRIPPLING ACADEMIC COSTS

In a recent survey conducted by the College Board, a student in the academic year of 2014-2015 paid in-state tuition amounting to $23,410. That's considered "moderate," and covers only *public schools.* The private school average for that same year was $46,272.

What if you have two kids? Three? Four?

STUDENT LOANS

An article by U.S. News reported this more than troubling statistic: "About 70 percent of 2013 graduates left college with an average of $28,400 in debt." Over *two thirds* of all college graduates finished school with nearly thirty thousand dollars in debt? That is, in a word, astounding. And that figure doesn't even take into account those students who *did not graduate.* Many of these students will have taken on astronomical levels of personal debt as well.

When factor in interest rates, and the next steps which are to rent an apartment, or put a down payment on a car or home, it's no real wonder at all why so many young people are crushed beneath the burden of debt. Starting a career in this way is similar to trying to play soccer with a broken knee: it can be done, but you are at a severe disadvantage.

These trends, by the way, show no signs of alleviation. Instead, more rain will come long before any possible ray of sunshine pierces these clouds.

MASTER'S DEGREES, DOCTORATES, DEGREES IN LAW AND MEDICINE

Extend the costs of attending an institution of higher education, drag out the loans and assume a "moderate" level institution is selected. These conditions could easily double the cost of earning a graduate degree or any other program requiring credits beyond those necessary to achieving a Bachelor's. Of course, the cost depends on the school. The average is not the be-all-end-all. The finer institutions of higher learning in this country accordingly charge steeper premiums for the privilege of attending.

As with those folks who graduate with a Bachelor's Degree, those who earn a Master's or above are by no means guaranteed a job once they are ready to head out into the world. And that's just a job. Finding or creating a situation in which one is gainfully and meaningfully employed is another matter altogether.

I highly doubt anyone would claim that the road to fulfillment in life begins with $60,000 or more in student debt.

Credit Card Debt

Given the citations above, one way in which Americans "are flunking the basics of personal finance" is clear for all to see. This quote comes from a CBS article which goes on to reveal that a net increase of $57.1 billion in credit card debt has been incurred by American households. Let me repeat that: this ridiculous number accounts only for *new* credit card debt, taken on in the year of 2014.

Put another way, the average household holds about $7,200 in debt, or $1,100 shy of an amount deemed to be completely "unsustainable."

Foreclosures Everywhere

The FDIC reports that, nationwide, "1 out of every 200 homes will be foreclosed upon" and "Every three months, 250,000 new families enter into foreclosure." Nearly half (43 percent) of American households spend more than they earn each year, and 42 percent don't own enough assets to keep themselves afloat for three months.

LIFESTYLE CHOICES

The previous point concerning foreclosures and spending ought to make the fact that Americans are not doing well abundantly clear. I am putting it mildly, of course.

Though what I am about to say is not true in all cases, to a significant degree, the decisions made by the individuals in question dig them deeper into the ditches within which they are stuck (if not landing them there in the first place). Buying or leasing a new car, taking on new entertainment expenses each month, accruing the latest accessories, shelling out the funds for a down payment on a home way outside their budgets...

"Unsustainable" is really the only word for these practices. Whether they are doing it to "keep up with the Joneses" or some other misguided notion, many Americans simply live beyond their means. Thus, they rob themselves of the potential to develop true, lasting wealth and achieve financial independence.

WORKING LATE INTO YOUR SEVENTIES

Does not sound like a barrel of laughs, now does it?

The American Dream of yore has crumbled above us, even as we reached to touch it. The illusion that you can still rely on a "steady," "good" job with "great benefits" and a "solid" pension is utterly outdated. This chapter has brought that much across, I hope. But all is not lost.

There is another way.

Because of all of the above-mentioned points, the future looks bleak for the American workforce.

You knew this already, you sensed it, or else you would not have opened this book and read up to this point. To reward you for your patience, here is some good news: you won't have to work into your seventies.

There is Another Way, A Better Way

In fact, following the guidelines set forth in this book could see you through to an early retirement. Or maybe you will enjoy your new line of work, the business you build from the ground up, running your investment portfolio to such a degree that you won't *want* to stop when you hit seventy.

For you, the American Dream can be reborn. You need not succumb to the cycle of spending and debt that has transformed the dream into nightmare. Moving forward, you can learn the lessons and acquire the tools you need to invest in your future and build your own career, characterized by true financial independence.

From here on out, it's all about what you can make happen. To begin this process of discovery, let's talk about the New American Dream.

2.

THE NEW AMERICAN
DREAM

We discussed the downfall of what I call the Old American Dream in the last chapter. The fact that you have diligently kept on reading indicates that you have the strength within you to discard the old in favor of something much better.

Remember the sheep, mindlessly bleating as they pursue banal lives rife with disappointment and hardship? By demonstrating the initial mental fortitude required to absorb the bad news of that first chapter, you are well on your way to rising to the challenges that are coming up. The road to true financial freedom is fraught with many dangers but, with the proper guidance, you will be as well prepared as you possibly can be to escape the drudgeries that will claim and defeat the vast majority of Americans.

Now, how would anyone go about getting their fair share in the middle of this era of fast-moving, digital money that simply can't be pinned down? What are the avenues down which one should drive to find the surest, fastest way to that tranquil garden known as prosperity? In short, what is the New American Dream?

The Story of the New American Dream

Once upon a time, a good, earnest person graduated from high school with good, earnest grades with hopes of being admitted to a good, earnest college. Thereafter, as you might imagine, such a person would land a good, earnest job. He would work, earnestly, for decades, building a pension, contributing to Social Security. Finally, at retirement age, he would leave his job, his former colleagues seeing him off with a gold watch and smiles all around. This individual would spend time tending his garden, sit with his wife in front of the TV, play with his grandkids and, overall, pass a pleasant few final years before his life ended.

This earnest, hard-working, fundamentally good person is an example of the American ideal of the last century. Said ideal persists to this day, probably because it did work for so many people for several decades. This was the era that began with the advent of our nation's global empire, which first took root at the turn of the century. In fact, the 1900s encompass what historians refer to as "The American Century," an epoch during which the United States was the forerunner militarily, politically and economically.

The problem is, the game has changed. There is no financial security provided by pensions or Social Security. Social Security, in reality, is projected to implode. The projected date of death varies depending on the source, but just about everyone agrees that this program, created in the 1940s under President Franklin Delano Roosevelt's administration, is outdated and doomed to fail. Those who refuse to agree that the current system is in disarray are fooling themselves and, in the end, they will be the ones who suffer most for their own ignorance.

There is No Security

The sooner you accept that you, and only you, are responsible for your financial security, the sooner you will be able to realize your dreams of financial independence. You will never have to work for the man again if you begin early, now, as soon as humanly possible, putting your money to work for you.

Do not make the mistake of relying on antiquated social safety nets. These will not save you when push comes to shove.

But You Hold the Power Within You

You can affect the changes that need to come about in order to free yourself from the bondage of the old, dying system. How?

By becoming an entrepreneur.

The America of the twenty-first century is the most thriving place in the world for the self-motivated, can-do sort of person. If you have a clear, defined goal and apply a little bit of know-how, you can turn your small, steady investments into a financial juggernaut in just a few years.

We will cover this subject in greater detail throughout the book, but you should know now that when you work for a company, you are not maximizing your potential. Really, you are working first for your corporate master, next your governmental master and, lastly, yourself. Eight hours a day of grueling menial tasks and a huge chunk of that is ripped out of your bimonthly check long before the paper ever touches your fingers. Even if you actually enjoy your job alright, you are still working for "the man," the "taxpayer," "Uncle Sam," or whatever moniker you would prefer to ascribe to the system that fleeces you of your earnings well before you even see the figure in the statement.

When you serve the same entity for years and years on end, as you were maybe told to do by your parents, grandparents, friends and family, you are exactly that: a slave. You may be well-paid on paper, but, at the end of the day, a large piece of your pie is snatched from your hand. You are to salivate over crumbs and are told to be grateful, too. That's the worst injustice of all: you are meant to thank those who are robbing you for the service they provided you.

If this outrageous you, you are far from alone. The difference between you and the angry, though largely ignorant majority, is that you are taking pains to educate yourself.

That is precisely why you are optimally suited for the entrepreneurial life.

TAKE A LOOK BEHIND THE "CURTAIN"

Prepare yourself for the following statement. Believe me, it's a doozy of a revelation. You have likely already intuitively come to grasp this idea, even if you have not yet put it to words. There is one thing you must understand and absorb before proceeding. Here is the truth about corporate America and, though there are always exceptions to any given rule, this statement applies to virtually all cases and scenarios:

When you work for someone else, you work to build their dream, not yours.

In the 1939 film *The Wizard of Oz*, it takes the instincts of the dog Toto to reveal to Dorothy and her friends, Scarecrow, Tin Man and the Lion, that the titular character is something of a sham. This peddler of tricks relied on illusion to aggrandize himself and belittle his subjects. Dorothy and company were made meek and lost the will to struggle against the wizard, until Toto intervened.

WE ALL HAVE THAT TOTO INSTINCT INSIDE OF US

It's true, we are all endowed with a desire to do well, to fight against tyranny. That instinct is what made America great. That same instinct is what has made possible the success of the few over the many servile, meek individuals populating this country. Where the latter shrivel in the face of despotism, the former consistently outsmart these tyrannical forces. The best part is that they do it using the very tools instituted by the system.

Let's stop being vague, shall we? We are, of course, talking about the government's proclivity to tax, tax, tax and spend, spend, spend money its representatives did not earn. The voracious appetite of our government grows with each passing year. It will never once shrink. The government is not prepared to go on a diet anytime soon. The law, written by Congressmen, of course, tells them that they are in the right. They have the "power of the purse" and dangle its authority over us every year during tax season. They will never stop taking "a piece of your action," as the saying goes. They are, in essence, doing what you must do. You must learn to do what seems logically impossible: create something from nothing, create money from no money.

Think about it for a minute. Is that not exactly what the government does through its tax code? Well, there's good news. You can harness that power and use it to pull your portfolio of investments onward and upward. To achieve that end, you will have to arm yourself with the knowledge and know-how to use the tax system to your advantage.

In the above paragraph, I was making use of colorful language like "despotism" and "tyranny" in hopes of invoking that unique spirit of American Exceptionalism that built our country. My aim was to awaken to an even greater degree the growing potential energy within you. Soon, you will be able to harness that energy.

How? Well, as an individual you are weak. I am sorry to put it so bluntly, but it's true. You have no real power to stand against the tax man as you are now. He knows where you live. He can find you and take his cut, no matter what. He has an army of lawyers and bureaucrats itching to watch you squirm.

But you can build a mirror of that same structure. Incorporate and become more than you are now. Only then can you be truly free.

Easier said than done, am I right? This is the first of many points in time in which I will tell you to erase that part of you driven to self-doubt. Starting a business is not impossible. It's not even the only way to make big money and escape "the rat race." It is *a* way, one of a few we will cover in this book. To capitalize on this opportunity, however, you must break away from the little voice telling you to "stop," "give up." Contrary to its assurances that "you can't do it" and "you will fail," you have all you need to begin defining your own life on your own terms.

"Your "I CAN" is more important than your IQ."

- Robin S. Sharma

Let's get started down the path of the entrepreneur.

THE STORY OF ENTREPRENEURSHIP

The simplest possible definition of an entrepreneur, and, coincidentally, the one I like most to use, is someone who builds their own dreams, rather than the dreams of another.

At your dead-end service industry job, you are working long, hard days to enrich the owners of the business.

At your corporate job, you are feeding money into the hands of the entrepreneurs who started or currently run that business.

No matter where you are, no matter the point in your career, if you do not own *assets* you own *nothing*. And if you own nothing, you work for others. There's much more to come on asset ownership, so keep reading.

Here is a statistic for you, from Forbes.com:

"Nonemployers" (those businesses that have annual business receipts of $1,000 or greater and are subject to federal income tax) have average revenues of $44,000.

To be clear, the Small Business Administration (SBA) defines a "small business" as an entity employing fewer than 500 people.

Imagine owning several nonemployer corporations. Talk about a no-nonsense revenue stream. The best part is, you will eventually be using your take from the companies you own to *buy more companies.* You will also be buying other types of investments, but now I am getting ahead of myself.

Not yet seeing why you should be impressed? That's fine. Here is a pair of facts for your consideration. Entrepreneur.com cited the IDC's study which, in 2004, determined the average annual revenue of a small business to be $3.6 million. That average swells to $5.03 million for those businesses who operate a website. Be aware that the IDC, an International Data Group subsidiary, classifies a business with fewer than 100 employees as "small."

This time, imagine being the owner of a couple or a few businesses of that caliber. I trust that I have earned your attention at this point.

A more current example comes to us through Chron.com, and I quote, "Small business owners with less than one year of experience in running an organization earn an annual salary ranging from $34,392 to $75,076." Now, *that* is something to write home about.

Of course, top performers, those small businesses that are run by shrewd, seasoned owners, can earn ten times the figures cited above. In all honesty, there are small businesses out there that bring in an annual take of over a million dollars or more. Granted, these are the exceptional few, but you could find yourself among their number sooner and easier than you might think. And, even failing to make millions off a single business, you may well earn hundreds of thousands of dollars to reinvest.

We have clearly found where the New American Dream was hiding. The time has come to grab it while we can.

THE NEW AMERICAN DREAM RISES FROM THE ASHES OF THE OLD

No doubt, you are asking the question, "How can I get this domino effect working for me?" You may have phrased it more eloquently, but the sentiment is something to which I can very much relate. Worry not, the answers are coming. Since we have established the necessity of becoming an entrepreneur, we can move forward.

Because I firmly believe in standing on the shoulders of giants, we are going to lean on a very well-respected work for the next few sections. Robert T. Kiyosaki's books, *Rich Dad Poor Dad and Rich Dad's Cashflow Quadrant: Guide to Financial Freedom,* are great resources for the budding entrepreneur.

Kiyosaki is an entrepreneur himself, but he is also an author and teacher who shows others how they might follow in his footsteps. He is a fabulous example of that quintessential American can-do spirit.

Through anecdotes and stories from his childhood and early adulthood, Kiyosaki's wonderful, little book, *Rich Dad Poor Dad,* relates a crucial lesson from the very beginning. He drives it home again and again. So, we may as well start there.

CHANGE THE WAY YOU THINK ABOUT MONEY

"The man who does not read has no advantage over the man who cannot read."

- Mark Twain

At its most abstract, the reason why so many Americans fail to capitalize on their immense potential is basic *financial illiteracy.* Just as those who cannot read are deprived of many of the advantages our society has to offer, one who is financially illiterate can never hope to make money.

If you cannot understand the rules of the game, you will never win.

The only possible exception to this rule is through the reliance on sheer, dumb luck. Relying on luck, however, will see you stay blind, deaf and mute when it comes to the dynamic world of interplaying financial forces.

Those familiar with Chaos Theory understand that, when seen from above, each individual random event fits into a much larger and incredibly intricate pattern. A similar set of forces come into play in the financial sphere. There is an order to what so many perceive as incomprehensible, random chaotic episodes. Following the threads of order within the tangle of chaos will allow you to espy, before anyone else does, where the trail will lead. Then, you will be ideally suited to capitalize on the opportunity presented.

Many, many folks, however, will drown in the waters of destitution. They were never taught the rules of the game, and thus they can never hope to win.

What are the rules? We'll get to them all eventually, but here is the most important one:

Pay yourself first.

You have heard this refrain before, probably. Like so many valid pieces of advice floating around amid the dregs and dross of bad advice, this statement is bafflingly simple. It appears so simple, in fact, that many shrug it off without giving it a second thought. You are no such person. You are here to learn the secrets and open new doors.

What does it mean to *pay yourself first?* The idea is intimately linked to another adage you may have picked up somewhere, "poor people work and rich people *make* money." Think about the word "make" for a moment. Think about its literal meaning. How can you make money? How might you make money behave as you want it to (i.e. have it make *more money* for you)?

To answer these questions, let's look at how the majority of Americans use their money. That order of operations is, by and large, as follows:

1. Work for wages or a salary (which is taxed)
2. Pay bills and mortgage, buy food, accrue material luxuries (which are taxed)
3. Pay taxes
4. OPTIONAL: Put a little away in the bank, or (even less likely) invest

The reason why bills, food and luxuries are all lumped into the same line is that these are usually given the same degree of consideration.

THE POOR AND MIDDLE CLASSES ARE TRAPPED IN A CYCLE

Work, buy, pay taxes. Repeat into infinity, and there you have the vicious spending cycle that grips the vast majority of American society today.

Say you work at an office as a receptionist, and you bring home a tidy $36,000 a year. Though one could certainly do better, that figure might look alright to some. But it is only an illusion, alas. No less than 15 percent of that will be eaten up solely by Social Security and Medicare taxes. You might think that number should be closer to 7.5 percent, but consider that this hypothetical receptionist's employer has to *match* that 7.5 percent. Thus, those dollars that could have gone to this imaginary employee instead flood the common pool. (And we have seen earlier in this book how generations of Americans are likely to never see a dime of those contributions returned to them when they need it most. Once you retire, you are on your own.) We haven't even accounted for State and Federal income taxes yet, by the way.

So, taxes are obviously a big drain on the earning potential of the American worker. But what about spending?

Big Macs, Bills, Mortgages and Buys

Expenses constitute another kind of drain on the wallets of middle class and poorer Americans. Of course, everyone has to eat. And, of course, no one is suggesting you let the water bill alone until your supply is completely cut off. But what is crucial to prolonged financial health is understanding that living within one's means is the only way to accrue long-term, lasting wealth.

In no way do Kiyosaki or I mean to sound callous when we state that very few people actually live within their means. Do you remember how it is unwise to "keep up with the Joneses?" Unfortunately, this is the exact sort of behavior that dominates the collective unconscious. Rather than investing their incomes, many families choose to funnel all of their earned cash into expensive luxuries like new gadgets, new cars and new homes. With all of these purchases comes a lasting price tag. Almost no one takes into account the nature of depreciation.

A car is automatically worth only three quarters of the price you paid for it as soon as the tires hit the road following the sale. Owning a piece of property that does not generate an income for you should, at long last, be considered for what it is: a liability. Take a moment to write up all the expenses involved in the proper maintenance of a home. A sampling of these expenses includes the need for a new roof every ten years (thousands of dollars), gutter cleanings (hundreds of dollars), frequent air conditioner maintenance and replacement (thousands of dollars), landscaping costs (hundreds of dollars), homeowner's association dues (hundreds of dollars per year), and gas, electric and water bills. Owning a home is starting to look a bit like a sort of financial deathtrap, isn't it?

Now, don't take away the false lesson that you should not invest in property. That is not at all the message of this chapter or this book. Yes, you and your family will have to live somewhere. The only distinction I am trying to draw is this: *view your family home as a liability*. It costs you money that could instead have been invested.

Because that lesson runs counter to conventional wisdom, only a select few will actually pay it any mind. It just so happens, however, that those who do take heed and reshape their mental outlook on property accordingly stand to benefit immensely.

The same must be done for bills and food costs. You must limit your expenses down to a manageable minimum and invest the rest in assets. Anything you buy, as you know, will be taxed. Thus, anything you buy is a liability. You pay for each item, like a car or computer, twice at the time of purchase (the price sticker with the added sales tax). The secondary invisible cost of owning these items is depreciation. A car or computer or cell phone will depreciate in value over time. That fact is as certain as the law of gravity's grip.

The truth of the matter is that, despite appearances to the contrary, the rich are not the only ones buying luxury items. The rich who stay rich are the only ones buying luxury items they can *afford*, that much is accurate. But, in reality, the middle class and even the poorer class spend their money as fast as it can come in. Oftentimes, they will spend it faster.

WHAT GETTING A RAISE MEANS TO MOST

The average middle class family's debt has been established in the chapter preceding this one. Why is it so steep? Why is individual debt so powerful as to be able to hold the majority of American households in its deathly talons?

In many cases, the answer is a lack of self-discipline. That may sound harsh, but how many folks do you know who put down payments on those new cars on the very day they learned they were getting raises? To most Americans, being given a raise triggers a small voice at the back of their minds telling them that they now have *more money to spend.* They now have more dollars to throw at restaurants, cars, boats, renovating their kitchens or building a "man cave" in the basement.

Why So Few "Have Money to Invest"

Well, it's not rocket science or anything. They *spend* it all as soon as it ends up in their hands or in their bank accounts. They spend the fraction of their earnings that remains once the tax vultures have picked them almost clean. Between the costs of bills and mortgages and the *desire* for status symbols, it's no wonder that all the money is so quickly used up. As soon we take hold of the latest check, many of us have already thought up ways to dispose of that income.

> "When obstacles arise, you change your direction to reach your goal, you do not change your decision to get there."
>
> *- Zig Ziglar*

There are those who, often far too late, choose to put money away in the bank. The decision to "save" is usually made during a time of crisis, or directly before one. For example, a couple preparing for the costs of putting their kids through college (see Chapter 1) may find they will have nothing left for their retirement. They might spend a few frantic years scraping together whatever scraps they can, but it all seems too little too late. And, more often than not, the preferred "solution" to impending destitution is let trickle a portion of each paycheck (after food, entertainment, bills and taxes) into a savings account.

A savings account, however, is almost as bad as keeping rolls of cash in your mattress. Why? One word: *inflation.* Over the last few decades, the standard rate of inflation has been around 2 percent, give or take. What does the typical savings account generate for you in terms of interest? *A fraction of one percent.* A "good" interest rate is 0.9 percent. So, by holding your money in a bank, the value of your earnings is *shrinking* every year.

Furthermore, pensions are hardly capable of saving the average employee from destitution in the latter years of his life. If they even live long enough to enjoy the pension, there is no guarantee that it will have survived.

DRIVING WITH THE TANK NEAR EMPTY

After accounting for all of the expenses listed and explained above, the average American will have nothing or less than nothing (college loans, credit card debt and so on). In short, they have only a few drops falling from a leaky faucet to quench their deadly thirsts.

Saving and investing were listed as "optional" earlier because that's how they are viewed, as tasks to complete *after* any and all other uses for money have been pursued. Who could have any money left to invest or save when, every half dozen years or so, the family feels the compulsion to upgrade its living arrangements? No, really, many American families fritter away lifetimes of earnings never *owning* anything, because they always need to move into a bigger, better more luxurious home. This makes paying off a 30 year mortgage utterly impossible. After all, someone who does this is selling property they don't own to put a down payment on a more expensive piece of property that they will never own, either.

Kiyosaki defines wealth as *"a person's ability to survive so many number of days forward — or, if I stopped working today, how long could I survive?"* (author's emphasis). This definition keys in on the fact that true wealth lends its owner *stability.*

With so many folks driving their metaphorical cars through life while their gas tanks are dangerously close to empty, how long do you imagine the typical American family could hack it if Dad or Mom (or both) lost their job?

Living paycheck to paycheck, or close to it, means that you will be in deep, deep trouble should the source of income cease. (And, in this economy, layoffs are all too common.)

They Have No Residual Income

Residual income is the term applied to any income leftover after debts (including the mortgage) are paid. Lenders, such as banks, calculate a potential borrower's residual income, factoring their findings into their final decision. There is however another definition of residual income and that is getting paid forever on work you did one time. Let me say it another way, ***do the work one time now and get paid for the rest of your life!*** We will cover residual income in greater detail later on. Suffice to say, for the moment, that this metric is critical to monitoring the pulse of your finances. Doing so will set you apart from the masses and give you the edge you need.

There are some other aspects, twists and turns to residual income, but we will save these for next chapter.

Speaking of developing an edge, if savings accounts are no good, where should you keep your money? The short answer is "lots of places." Let's look at the longer, more useful answer.

Building a Business is Building an Asset Column

The comprehensive answer to the question "where should I invest my money?" can transform you into a true entrepreneur and give you the means to become independently wealthy.

We have arrived back at the concept of "paying yourself first." You have now seen the ways in which many folks choose to pay themselves *last*. The time has come to flip the process on its head.

Where most Americans follow this process:

1. Earn money
2. Spend money (bills, mortgage, car payments, food, etc.)
3. <u>IF POSSIBLE</u>: Put money into a savings account

The successful entrepreneur's order of operations looks like this:

1. Earn money
2. Invest money
3. Spend money
4. Investments earn money
5. Reinvest money
6. Rinse and repeat

That is the secret to *paying yourself first*. By investing the bulk of your residual income, pressure builds up behind the dam. Eventually, that dam will burst and money will flow forth in gushing streams.

It may look like the investor's path is twice as long, but do not be fooled. With a bit of careful, intelligent management of step five, steps four and six become almost automatic. This is what it means to *make* money. You now know the process by which the rich get and stay rich.

Your business, as an investing entrepreneur, will be to buy real estate, businesses and anything else that might interest you and off of which you can make a buck. There are nearly infinite opportunities out there. Explore and let exciting possibilities catch your eye. Just remember, you are not buying *liabilities*. Instead, you will be buying assets.

Building a Business is Building an Asset Column

If you have ever perused a balance sheet, you will be familiar with the difference between assets and liabilities. These are divided into two neat columns. The latter contains items like the home mortgage, the credit card balances, student and car loans and so on, while the former should reflect only those items that generate value for you, their owner.

That last part was subtle, so let me repeat it more clearly. Your assets column should *not* include your home, your car and other such items. Why, you ask? We have already reviewed the myriad ways in which a house can bleed you dry. It should come as no big shock that a car is much the same. Wear and tear, gas prices and interest payments are a few of the many concerns that are tied to owning a vehicle. The fact that it depreciates by 25 percent as soon as it leaves the car lot should be taken to heart, as well. Therefore, neither your home nor your car should be counted among your assets, even though the IRS might tell you otherwise. They are liabilities, costing you varying amounts of money on a regular and/or semi-regular basis.

Real assets, according to Kiyosaki, include:

• Businesses you own but don't need to manage
• Stocks
• Bonds
• Real estate that generates income
• Intellectual property royalties
• Notes (IOUs), contracts between buyer and seller (bypassing the banks)

Investigating which businesses you should buy, or starting your own, involves properly identifying a niche market and seizing the opportunity to build wealth.

Remember, it's all a game. You may win a round, or you may come up short. But, as long as you learn from your mistakes, you will emerge ready for the next challenge stronger than ever before.

Kiyosaki teaches students in an effort to pass on his investing and management skills, developed over a lifetime of learning. He rightly makes yet another excellent point when he states, to paraphrase, that the education system in this country has got its hat on backwards. Think back to your college or high school days. Picture the faces of all those "A students," those academic high-achieving *wunderkinds.* Maybe some of them emerged from the ivory tower of academia better for their book learning and ready to face the world head on. However, it is clear that earning high grades, while a worthy pursuit, *on its own* is no guarantee that an individual will do well in the wide world beyond the campus.

Formal education will make you a living; self-education will make you a fortune.

- Jim Rohn

Many geniuses are so specialized that they have trouble dealing with those who do not share their particular world views. Therefore, the generalist — he or she who knows a little about a wide range of subjects — can get ahead on the steam of such individuals. In other words, social intelligence is vital to the entrepreneurial spirit. Add to that a bit of sound guidance, a love of learning and a willingness to experiment, and you have a recipe for great success.

CLASS DIFFERENCES

This is a very useful and easy to remember breakdown Kiyosaki gives to illustrate the differences between the classes:

- The poor have only expenses
- Members of the middle class buy liabilities they think are assets
- Rich people buy assets

As noted in Kiyosaki's book, the real victim, by all appearances, is the middle class. They foot the largest bill to cover the costs inherent in contemporary American society, a society that has reinforced their desires for luxuries they cannot reasonably afford. Many of these individuals, in an effort to appear wealthier than they are, leverage their credit cards to the breaking point in order to buy a newer car or larger home. The result is crippling debt from which they will likely not escape without years or decades of hard work. Many will not escape at all.

Government taxation brutalizes the middle class, who must support the bloated operations of the ruling body on their overtaxed backs. The wealthy have many resources available to them to help them protect their assets: from lawyers held on retainer, who know the ins and outs of the absurdly complex tax code, to stock brokers, who can manage accounts in such a way as to keep them all but untouchable.

On the other hand, the middle class has no safety net, unlike the poor who might at least receive entitlements like Medicaid and unemployment checks. If a middle class family hits choppy waters, its members have no recourse until they become poor themselves. This result is, for obvious reasons, undesirable.

That's one way out of the middle class. I am sure you would prefer the alternative: becoming rich. If you want to be rich, you have to act it. Therefore, buy *assets* to fill your column. These, in turn, will generate revenue with which you can buy *more* assets. Eventually, this new cycle will be self-sustaining and you will have brought about a rebirth of the American Exceptionalism. Like a phoenix rising from the ashes, the New American Dream will be born from the old.

To embed yourself in the upper class, you should be aware of another very useful tool.

THE CASHFLOW QUADRANT™

In Kiyosaki's book, *Rich Dad's Cashflow Quadrant*, he outlines the different sources of income available to a given individual. These are "E" for employee, "S" for small business owners or those who are self-employed, "B" for big business and "I" for investor.

Throughout the book, Kiyosaki details the various directions cashflow might take. Where to and wherefrom the flow is headed depend on both the predilections and education of the wage-earner.

Before continuing, let's take a look at the diagram below.

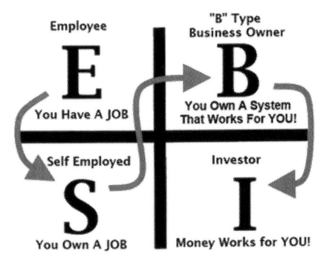

Traditional schools — especially public ones, but private institutions are culpable often enough — instill a particular brand of values in our children. We learned it, too, believe it or not. We are all taught from an early age to obey the teacher, get good grades, earned the diploma and then the degree and, finally, land and hold a job. We are told this is the right, honest way to lead one's life, that it produces value for society.

The question is, who is reaping the rewards of that added value? If you are not yet rich from your efforts, the answer clearly is not "I reap the rewards of my labor."

Kiyosaki's own experiences teaching have shown him that much instructors advocate focusing on the E and S quadrants. This is especially true when we are talking about so-called financial education. Kiyosaki, ever contrarian to the status quo, tells us that his "rich dad" advised focusing on the B and I quadrants. Whether you have to work your way up, or you can start there straightaway, ending up anywhere else will only keep you fettered to a relentless system that does not care about you or your family. You will remain a good, little worker bee, busily packing away honey for the queen's consumption. Forget about ever having any honey of your own.

KEEP READING IF THAT FATE DOESN'T APPEAL TO YOU

Let's define our terms here:

- Falling in the E quadrant means *you have a job*
- S means *you own a job*
- B is a system operated by people who *work for you*
- I is money *working for you*

Clearly, the way to become rich, quickly and legitimately, is to exploit the resources of *other people's time* and *other people's money.*

Being employed, or even self-employed, means your maximum energy output is limited to yourself and those immediately surrounding you. That's why an E and S focus, even if wonderfully managed, can never be as successful as its counterpart: the B and I.

You should, of course, keep your day job. Quitting it will cut off the initial source of income, holding your engine stuck in second gear. If you leave your job too early and you have not started investing, you will obviously never get anywhere at all.

HOLD ONTO YOUR E

Your job is a means to an end. If your goal is to leave it, you certainly can. You only need to wait until your money-making engine is self-sustaining. Meaning, your assets generate enough revenue to cover *all* of your liabilities *and then some*. It stands to reason that having enough free cash to invest is critical to growing your wealth.

The ultimate objective of your use of the *Cashflow Quadrant*^{TM} is to have less than 30 percent of your income generated from your E job. The other 70 percent or greater should be coming from your I, your investments. This destination is within your reach. You are well on your way, in fact!

WHAT YOU DON'T WANT TO DO

You risk poverty at the slightest unexpected turn of events when you rely on your E or S jobs for 80 percent or more of your income. Having only 20 percent awaiting you from investments (if you even have it at all) can be disastrous. Pensions can evaporate in the wake of a corporation's financial troubles. Or the investments, even if "successful," can bear little fruit after years of sitting in that mutual fund.

To be blunt about it, you can't be averse to risk. Fear is your greatest enemy and it walks hand-in-hand with self-doubt. If you fear risk, you will never be in a position to seize unique opportunities as they present themselves.

> **"Our doubts are traitors and make us lose the good we oft might win by fearing to attempt."**
> *-William Shakespeare*

Refusing to flirt, on occasion, with risk leads to "playing it safe." We have spent a lot of time discussing how well that works out for most Americans. Now, should you go out and put everything in small cap stocks or international funds? Of course not. But you must understand that every investment, including real estate, bears some degree of risk. It falls to you to assess your options and tailor the size of your position accordingly.

What You Do Want to Do

Move through all of the quadrants, funneling more and more money into I and B. The worst thing you could do is stay stuck in E or even S forever, running in circles. The only accomplishment you will be able to claim at the end of that vicious cycle is the groove your footfalls dug into the floor beneath your old and tired feet. Don't spend an eternity chasing job after job. Keep your E job and use the resources you gain to move into I and B.

To the uninitiated, the world of I is a frightening labyrinth. Really, though, getting started is not nearly as terrible as it seems. For one thing, a diverse portfolio is your shield against investments which bear more inherent risk. Since there are many works written on this very subject, we will not cover it in detail in this book. We will instead provide you with management solutions to help you throughout your career of pursuing personal enrichment, beginning in the upcoming Chapter 3.

In the meantime, remember that the most important thing you can do is to enjoy the process. Think of investing as a game. You win some and you lose some, learning all the while. When you live to learn, you won't be able to stop yourself from improving.

In the next chapter, we will discuss *how* to get your money to work for you!

3 .

TRANONT: A COMPANY DEDICATED TO HELPING AMERICANS

We have arrived, at last, at that fated moment. You are at a crossroads in your life. Two paths lie before you. On the left, you have the way you have been going throughout the entirety of your existence. That way leads to sticking it out in that job you despise for years on end. That road is known to you because you have never stopped walking it. You see yourself dwindling as you go, shuffling through the dust, turning into dust yourself even as you put one foot before the other. Each step is full of resentment. Each footfall's hollow echo is seared into your mind as you search desperately to turn back, knowing full well that you cannot. There is only forward.

Because you can only move forward in life, you are bound by the decisions you make. But you don't have to choose the left path; that way promises only to be long and filled with sorrow. Today may well be one of the greatest, most pivotal days you will ever experience, because you have the chance to take the alternate path. Head right at this fork, and awaken to the New American Dream.

"Live for the future today and just forget
yesterday's sorrows...
Because when you open the present...
That's when you find your tomorrow...
They say 'tomorrow is always a day away'...
But I say that this is the day that I say bye to
yesterday and today..."

-Miguel Mendez

Always remember, going forward, that you need not walk this path alone. There are many potential allies to enlist. We are about to profile the first and foremost among them.

THE WAKING DREAM

For the brave among us, those who dare shirk the fetters of a broken system, there is assistance to be found. We who want to break free and achieve true financial independence can find powerful forces to aid us. We are about to review one such entity on which we might lean. I think you are really going to appreciate the company philosophy.

HELP YOURSELF, HELP OTHERS

In the previous chapter, we talked about doing right by you. You need to realize and deeply believe that you deserve material and spiritual success and happiness. Focusing on yourself, however, is only half of the equation. To solve for that "X element" missing from your life, as we are about to see, does not require you to neglect your drive to be a Good Samaritan in your community. Many people assume that they need to receive before they can give.

I am here to tell you that your personal, financial independence cannot come about in a vacuum. Nor should it! Doing right by yourself doesn't mean you can't also do right by others. There is myth prevalent in this country that to be rich, you must become vaguely and cartoonishly evil. That's frankly absurd. Every wealthy person does not receive a contract containing the clause "rub your hands together, snickering all the while, as you bamboozle a single mother and her five children out of their mobile home." This misperception has really done a number on America's collective psyche. Class warfare is a tragic byproduct of the perpetuation of this misguided mythology. This chapter will help you see how becoming wealthy and expanding the scope of your generosity of spirit can live under the same roof in harmony.

Some of the kindest, most generous people I know are those who have achieved true financial freedom. The number of dollars to your name does not color one's character in and of itself. Good people come from all walks of life, of course, but I have found that financial independence gives you the opportunity to set the terms of your own destiny and, therefore, achieve a much greater degree of happiness. And, when you are happy, you will have more energy to spread among your family, friends, community, city, nation and world. However, the process must begin with the recognition that, even as you rise, you can pull others up with you. Side by side, we can achieve much more than we can alone.

It is this ideal idea that embodies the spirit of Tranont, one company that is working tirelessly to help Americans achieve true financial freedom, long-term business success and, ultimately, personal fulfillment and happiness.

Change Your Life Rapidly

The name "Tranont" comes from the French word which translates to "change life rapidly." As you will see in the upcoming sections, this concept is integral to the philosophies of Tranont and Tranont Life (its sister company). Let's find out how you can rapidly shift the balance of power of the dynamic forces ruling your life. Take the time to parse the forthcoming details and you will soon harness the energies that once controlled you in order to assert authority over your own destiny.

Tranont stems from National Marketing Resources (NMR), which boasts over 20 years of delivering to clients world class consulting services. Over that time frame, NMR realized that so many of their clients were experiencing tax-related problems that drove them up a wall. Buried in debt, it was no wonder these folks could not build a plan on their own. In response, the goal of NMR has been and always will be to help the average American succeed beyond their wildest dreams.

From the shoulders of NMR, a nearly 2 billion dollar company, Tranont, was born. This company continues the proud legacy of its forbear, bringing solutions to the modern American, so that he or she can face down the challenges of the 21st century.

THE AUTHORITY

When deciding to learn about a brand new subject, I find it best to tap into the source itself. That's why Mr. Ron Glover is such a great resource for those of us who are looking to dedicate ourselves to building a business and realizing the New American Dream.

Glover is a fulltime, professional advertising, sales and marketing trainer working with Tranont. He is a driven self-starter and wants nothing more than teach you how you, too, can be as successful as he has become. Over the course of his illustrious career, he has built multiple businesses from the ground up. His watchwords are "motivation" and "drive," and he wants to see you embody these qualities as well.

Glover is passionate about your success. For this reason, he begins many of his lectures with the question, "Do you ever wonder what makes others successful?" This question actually has multiple aspects to it. Embedded within it are the subliminal queries of "how" and "why." Glover's lectures are available through Tranont on its website, on YouTube and other places around the World Wide Web. They are highly recommended for additional research purposes. Seek them out as soon as you get through this book.

To borrow a phrase from Glover, I invite you to "be present" as you read through the remainder of this work. Maybe that sounds a little bit hokey to you, but that should not be the case. All I am asking of you, at this juncture, is to open your mind and let the forthcoming information strike you as it will. Remember, it is important to dare to explore.

Alright, let's get down to business.

PEACE OF MIND

"Success means doing the best we can with what we have. Success is the doing, not the getting; in the trying, not the triumph. Success is a personal standard, reaching for the highest that is in us, becoming all that we can be."

-Zig Ziglar

Recognizing, as you have, that the old way of doing things is on its way out, you want to inhabit the New American Dream. You don't want to remain one of those desperately clinging to outdated and unreal notions of how to achieve stability. Furthermore, you want to help others achieve success even as you do, because community fosters strength.

Have you felt forced to abandon your dreams? In Chapters 1 and 2, we saw how and why so many Americans have been divorced from "peace of mind," or what Glover calls "the most valuable asset" available to any citizen of this country. Maybe you have maxed out a credit card or two, just trying to stay afloat during tough economic times. Maybe the depreciation of your car(s) and the devaluation of your home following the housing bubble have taken their toll on your checkbook. Know that it is going to be alright. Really, it is. Starting with this book, and moving to Tranont's side, you can restore yourself and your family to the glory days. In fact, you can far and away exceed your expectations for the future.

So, get your dreams back! Make these stressful years a distant memory you can someday laugh about while sipping fruity drinks from a resort beach in Bali. Find your peace of mind today with Tranont!

A UNIQUE BUSINESS OPPORTUNITY

According to Glover, there are two keys to earning lasting wealth. He goes on to say that, given the competitive economic landscape, "everybody needs financial solutions and education." Tranont's personal success mentors are in the business of providing Americans like you with exactly these tools. You have already begun the process of educating yourself by opening this book and pressing onward up to this point. That fact alone counts as a huge vote cast in favor of a brighter future for you. Now let's see what Tranont is offering you.

The two keys to wealth will be familiar to you from last chapter. But they bear a succinct statement:

1. *Start your own business.* When you own an operation, you liberate yourself from the bonds of hourly wages and salaries.
2. *Invest wisely, invest safely.* Easier said than done, which is why you need a team dedicated to your personal triumph.

In essence, Tranont is extending its hand to you. Before you lies that familiar fork in the road, and you know where the left path leads. The right one, however, leads to *partnership with Tranont.* Here's why that is such an exciting prospect.

BECOMING A TRANONT ASSOCIATE

Tranont has strategically partnered with dozens of major companies. These include National Processing, American National, Fidelity & Guaranty Life, Victig, Bliss Wireless, Jive Business Phones, Voya, and many more.

How powerfully could your financial situation be impacted by a partnership with such a company? No doubt the picture is beginning to form in your mind. If you are seeing dollar signs, I don't blame you.

There are no sales pitches. All costs are delineated up front. You can expect honesty and forthrightness in your every interaction with a Tranont representative. They really care about your wellbeing.

That does not mean that there isn't a little bit of tough love involved. Glover says it best: to succeed "takes skills, it takes learning, it takes education and personal development." Choosing the right path is stupidly simple. Walking it, well, that's a horse of a different color.

INVESTIGATING TRANONT

In the interest of full disclosure, I am a convert to the Tranont philosophy, as I believe you might soon be, too. Though I would not call my initial attitude "skepticism," *per se*, I did maintain a healthy investigative attitude when first approaching Tranont. At the time Tranont was introduced to me I was working 60 plus hours a week at my corporate job and running my own small business. I really didn't have any extra time. But when I realized what Tranont was doing I remembered something one of my mentors use to tell me, "nobody is too busy, it's just a matter of priorities". Well, I reprioritized.

What I found as I dug deeper was incredible. The raw potential they offer to the average American lit up my mind. I began to see how my despair over the death of the Old American Dream could be channeled into my will to bring about a new one. Tranont showed me how necessary it was to write this book, to spread the word of hope as far as possible.

I want nothing more than to see you infused with the same hope and zest for life that I discovered when I found Tranont. Together, we can uplift one another and build our New American Dream.

"THE PEOPLE'S FRANCHISE"

Tranont mission of serving the average American has labeled it "the People's Franchise." The sweeping change they embody is simply revolutionary. A tremendous shift in wealth is imminent, and you can be standing outside when the money flood is let loose.

A revolution will not get far without the right products. That's why Tranont has made available a suite of excellent tools and products for its associates. For a small monthly fee, you will gain access to the full functionalities reserved for Tranont partners: Tranont OneView, Tranont Tax, Tranont Defend, Tranont Life, Tranont Education, plus a wide variety of B2B services. "The People's Franchise" has geared up to give you everything you need to start a business, invest smartly and dominate your market.

Smart money management tools allow you track financial performance across a wide array of platforms. Protect your identity with exclusive software solutions, ensuring the security of your personal and financial information. Glover explains that, "Identity theft is one of the largest crimes in the world today" and "protect[ing] your online identity... is absolutely mandatory." These and more go a long way toward giving you the peace of mind you need when operating in this fast-paced, fickle digital market.

THE TOOLS OF THE TRADE

We will cover each of the upcoming entries in greater detail in Chapter 4, but I believe an overview of the tools of the trade is in order.

- Extreme PC Makeover, check-up, tune-up and lock up. With iCare PC you get an unlimited computer tech support plan and computer security service. "That's like having a Geek Squad at your house... 24 hours a day, 7 days a week."

- Tranont Life: Tranont's sister company provides investment solutions and guidance
  o Say you had invested $100,000 in the Standard & Poor's 500 in the year 1999. By the way, in case you were not aware, the S&P 500 is one of the most widely used stock market indexes. At any rate, if left alone from 1999 to present day, your $100,000 would currently be worth $125,000. Now, if you had followed Tranont Life's "Index Universal Life Policy," your $100,000 would now be $259,000." Again, both scenarios involved zero management on your part.
  o Your third option involves meeting with Tranont elite financial specialists. With their expert guidance, that same $100,000 invested at the turn of the new millennium would have reached $576,000. Glover and I both strongly recommend you take the third route, for obvious reasons.

- When you start your own business with Tranont, you will have approximately 150 different tax benefits and write-offs coming to you.
  o Did you know that the number one expense for most American households comes to you courtesy of the tax man? Most average Americans pay nearly 50 percent of their income in taxes" each year.
  o Track your expenses and manage all of your receipts.

- o Tranont's tax app tracks all of your possible deductions, simultaneously enriching you and keeping you audit-proof.
- o Thanks to the Cloud, all of your information is accessible by you (and only you) from anywhere on the globe.
- o According to Glover, "If you keep your records and file properly using a tax professional, and if you're an average income earner of $51,000 a year, owning your own business qualifies you to use about 150 tax deductions that will help you gain about $3,000 to $5,000 back per year on your taxes."

- The Smart Banking tool empowers you to eliminate debt through intelligent tax and investment strategies.

- Credit card processing services through National Processing give you the lowest rates, guaranteed. Screening solutions include a background check which is turned around in just 36 hours. All you need to do is fill out a form.
  - o Setting up this account gives you a source of *residual income*. For more information, see below.

- Your merchant account will be overseen and protected by national processing representatives who will call the client and close the deal for you, removing any need for worried micromanaging. Best of all, you get an additional 10 percent in *residual income* just for setting up this account.

- Tranont Marketing Platform:
  Just like everything else Tranont does, the myTranont website is cutting edge. The myTranont site is broken up into two main areas, the myTranont back office and the myTranont administration site.

myTranont Back Office

The myTranont Back Office is where individuals can direct prospects to help them gain a better understanding of Tranont, the OneView application and the business opportunity available to them.

Users that access this site are able to navigate through Tranont promotional videos, website content and downloadable PDF documents regarding product, compensation plans and the necessary details for the Tranont business opportunity. The site is broken up into main areas that can be accessed via the tabbed navigation.

myTranont Administration Site

The myTranont administration site is where associates go to manage the content displayed on the myTranont back office site. Not only does the site provide the ability to manage the various content options available from Tranont, users can also manage their list of contacts as well as any prospecting efforts that have taken place.

Site administrators can set up a variety of drip marketing campaigns and they can integrate with various social media applications. They can also set up task lists that generate notifications and reminders when a specific action needs to be taken.

The goal is to provide a system that helps automate some of the initial prospecting efforts to help you be more efficient in your business building efforts. Access to the myTranont site is provided with your monthly subscription.

These tools and more will find their way into your arsenal should you choose to enlist Tranont as your new business's partner.

A Note on the Importance of Education

Financial illiteracy is one of the leading factors landing Americans in dire financial straits. Thus, it is vital that you educate yourself concerning the possibilities lying at your feet. "Financial education is what separates the wealthy from everybody else," states Glover. The opportunities available to a small business through Tranont are "second to none." You can start your business tomorrow, thanks to franchising options. It does not take much to gain traction with "the People's Franchise" on your side.

Spreading the Word

In terms of allies to support your growing business, you need not limit yourself to Tranont. Once you have initiated your business venture by setting up an account with Tranont, you can talk up the services and opportunity to friends and acquaintances. For every referral you bring into the fold, you will earn *residual income*. It is even possible to generate substantial earnings on a part-time basis. With Tranont, spreading the word means spreading the wealth. But, this time, spreading the wealth makes you richer, too!

What follows is a brief illustration of how building a strong network through Tranont can help you achieve financial freedom. *Note that this compensation plan was in effect at the time of writing but may since have been improved upon by Tranont in order to increase the earning potential of its associates.*

Once you let three people know about the company and the great opportunities it gives them, if these three individuals start their businesses through Tranont, you will gain the rank of *Executive*. Your new title grants you $100 per month in *residual income*.

When these three new businesses generate income, you earn a percentage of *their* residual income streams. Should these three individuals each recruit three new partners, they will become Executives in their own right. That means that, with only 12 people under the wing of your growing organization, you will receive a cut of each *residual income*. In addition, by keeping these 12 people active, you will earn a Jeep bonus of $500 month. That's like getting a free Jeep whose only cost is your commitment to your own financial freedom. Your new Jeep will be three years old or newer. (And, if you do not happen to want a Jeep, you can instead opt for a $250 per month cash bonus).

Thus, by helping your associates find associates of their own, everybody wins. In all seriousness, how popular would you be in your neighborhood or social circle for setting up so many of your friends with this chance to be truly successful and happy? Let me tell you, it is rather difficult to be sullen and miserable while driving a Jeep. Especially a Jeep you received as a bonus for work well done, costing you nothing out of pocket.

There is no real limit to the amount of money you can earn in *residual income* through the referral domino effect. If you reach a higher rank, having recruited 25 people into your organization, you will earn $200 per month, plus the $500 for your new Jeep. Also, every single one of your members who owns a merchant account will give you a 1 percent override (the commission received by the sales manager – you!), putting another $250 dollars in your pocket.

Glover encourages you to invest in your future today with Tranont, stating that "There's actually millions of dollars available in this compensation plan." He warns, however, that you will need to be "focused" and think with your "long-term" goals in mind. This path does require dedication and mental fortitude.

Building a group of 10,000 associates, for example, would be far from easy. But Glover has achieved this level of success (and greater) multiple times throughout his career. To give you an idea of what you are shooting for, earning Tranont's CEO rank (i.e. having 10,000 associates in your organization) will give you $130,000. Not per *year,* but per *month*. Even if it took you ten years to reach that point, you will have grown and learned all along the way. And let's not forget how much money you stand to make even at the middling or lower rungs of the ladder.

Kiyosaki wrote that his poor dad taught him to climb the corporate ladder, the traditional advice given to the average American worker. His rich dad simply asked, "Why not own the ladder?"

With Tranont, you won't have to suffer a long, arduous climb. You can own the ladder to your success.

QUESTIONS TO ASK YOURSELF

Before proceeding, ask yourself if you are ready. Look within yourself to find that curious side of you, and use it to channel your hunger for change into a powerful force for good. You have a lot to look forward to, so keep that positive attitude going!

Due to your exhaustion, you have missed quite a few boats in your day. You owe it to yourself to not miss this one. Get in on the ground floor of Tranont's operation and watch your profits shoot through the roof and into orbit.

All you need to do is:

1. Fill out your application
2. Start your business ASAP (another pearl of Glover-wisdom: "The secret of getting ahead is getting started.")
3. Are you teachable and long-term thinking? Good! Tranont has all sorts of lessons available to the avid learner.

"It's your financial future," says Glover. "What do you want it to look like, and when" would you want to see those results develop? Tranont invites you to join its professional team because, "after all, the only thing missing is you." And Glover reminds you to "have some fun in life!"

WHAT DOES TRANONT STAND TO GAIN?

Aside from the modest fee for the plethora of services provided, Tranont's reward for helping so many Americans is the satisfaction of a job well done. And if that does not embody the spirit that once made America great, I don't know what could. At the end of a long day's work, you should be able to put your feet up and rest. The same goes for years of labor. If there seems to be no end in sight for you, if you feel stuck at your current job, you are relegating yourself to building the dreams of others. Why not focus, for once, on your own? Don't you deserve your piece of the action and the peace of mind living the New American Dream will bring?

Before rounding off this chapter with another quick look at the philosophy of generosity that animates Tranont, we are going to explore one more angle to this vision that is driving us ever onward.

ARE YOU TIRED OF GETTING NOTHING FOR SOMETHING?

You put in a lot of work, but, lately, you can only see that you are spinning your wheels in place, going nowhere. We have all been there at one point or another, don't worry. As long as you did not skip the above sections, you have already learned ways to build your future success starting today. (If you did skip or skim over them, I invite you take a closer look.)

For those who feel caught in the mud, tires grinding into the earth with no real hope of escape, there's a wonderful book, written by Kathleen Rich-New. It is entitled *Plan B: The Real Deal Guide to Creating Your Business.* When your Plan A is causing you so much distress and only landing you in ever greater debt, you need a Plan B, and Tranont can help you create one for all the reasons cited above. More importantly, Tranont gives you the tools you need to make your plan actionable.

No longer will you be forced to accept little-to-nothing for so much effort. Instead, materialize something out of nothing. It's not magic; it's Tranont.

We will soon look into some Plan B concepts that you can implement with Tranont as your stalwart partner. Investigating these components will show you how to apply Tranont's solutions to your particular situation. Soon enough you will find yourself living the New American Dream.

First, however, let's hit the bull's-eye on a few hurdles you will have to vault along the way.

THE LOYALTY TRAP

Working to fulfill the dream of another can spiral out of control quite quickly. Your employer might be expecting you to constantly work harder and faster for the same or near-enough-as-makes-no-matter pay. (Remember, if your raises don't exceed the rate of inflation, you are *losing money!*) The fact of the matter is, remaining loyal to a single company for years on end is the surest way to kill your chances of ever creating wealth.

THE EXPECTATIONS OF A MODERN LIFESTYLE

The modern average American has to cough up more money for bills than any previous generation. Internet, home phone, cell phone and satellite/cable are but a few examples of expenses over which your parents or grandparents simply did not have to concern themselves. With so much money flying out the window, who will pay those bills after you retire?

SOCIAL SECURITY AND RETIREMENT PLANS

You know it, you pay for it and it is the biggest (legal) paycheck thief out there. Social Security was implemented in 1935, back when reaching the ripe age of 65 was considered a noteworthy achievement. Today, many more Americans than ever before are expected to surpass that age (and easily). That's great news — we should all like to enjoy ourselves on this Earth just a little longer. This trend does, however, place a great deal of stress on the so-called social safety net.

Rich-New cites a statistic which claims Social Security will be completely bankrupt by 2036. Who knows what will happen at that point in time. Couple that frightening fact with the disintegration of traditional retirement plans (which never generated much revenue anyway, because investment funds never grow fast enough), and you have yourself a recipe for financial disaster. Even with defined contribution plans, which require vesting, you still have to abide the risk of being laid off, or seeing the company go belly-up.

It should be clear that relying on eventual handouts, from the government or your place of employment, is no safe bet whatsoever.

FEAR OF PAIN AND FAILURE

Of course, one of the most oppressive obstacles you will come up against is your own *fear*. Failing is a very real possibility. Something like 80 percent of all start-ups implode within a year or five, after all. You might fear losing the money you scraped together during years of grueling service to an employer you did not care much for at all.

Let me ask you this, though: given the choice of a potential set-back or a guaranteed miserable next couple to a few decades, which would you prefer? When you are your own boss, you set the parameters of your business and you determine how quickly you can bounce back from any backsliding. When you suffer under another's lash, you deprive yourself of the chance of claiming a better life.

Harness and use the fear of the latter case to drive yourself, full-speed into the dream of a brighter tomorrow.

Start with These Questions

Ask yourself:

1. Where do I want to be when I retire? What do I want my life to look like then?
2. What do I respect and value in myself, or in my chosen role models?
3. When was I last happy with my work?

Answering these questions can help you find the perfect Plan B to get you out of that rut you are in. Just know that there are no "wrong" choices, except the one where you stand still.

Move On

The first step of any journey is invariably the most difficult to make. Alleviate the stress of starting on a brand new path by creating a list of "wants" and "don't wants." What *do* you want to have happen with your finances, your personal life, your time with family? What *don't* you want?

Use your answers to the questions above as guides. To keep things positive, for every "don't want" you should add two or more "wants" to your list. Focus on where you want to end up, rather than where you are now or where you are headed. You will not be able to focus on turning your ship if you are fixated on the iceberg in the distance.

To change, you have to be *willing* to change. It all stems from your initial choice.

The Ingredients of Change

To enact meaningful change, you will need the following ingredients: a vision, the right skills, strong incentives, sufficient resources and a detailed action plan.

The most successful entrepreneurs in this country are those who embody utilitarianism and individualism, are theoretical-minded and, most importantly, *quick to change*. A pragmatic approach, bolstered by the can-do work ethic that built this country, should be suffused with a healthy love of theory. If you can't theorize, you can't imagine. And if you can't imagine, you can't innovate. Don't worry if one idea does not pan out the way you planned. Being adaptable will keep your eyes on the ball and ready for the critical interception.

SEEK OUT PROFESSIONAL MENTORS

> "You can make positive deposits in your own economy every day by reading and listening to positive, life-changing content, and by associating with encouraging and hope-building people."
>
> *- Zig Ziglar*

In line with Tranont's highest regard of education, you should ingratiate yourself to those who are more knowledgeable than you are. Find the expert in the industry you are trying to break into and ask how he developed his niche.

Always seek out new ways to train yourself and new teachers to educate you. Learning is not solely the province of children. Adults learn constantly, too. Therefore, make sure you are absorbing the knowledge, skills and techniques that will serve you best going forward. Furthermore, there is no reason why these talented teachers and mentors cannot become your allies.

As previously stated, *don't quit your day job* (what Kiyosaki referred to as your E or S job). Think of it this way: you are in school, but you still need to pay the bills and put money away. So you have to bite that bullet for the time being. But you can do anything, as long as it is temporary. Just keep your eyes on the prize and, before you know it, you will be waving a final "good-bye" to your former boss and colleagues.

Building a Plan B

Whether you are creating a business, purchasing an existing one, buying a franchise or slated to become a distributor, there are a good many aspects to consider when setting to the task of formulating your Plan B. These include:

- The number of dollars and hours required
- The risk involved
- The quantity and quality of training hours you have already undergone
- The quantity and quality of training available
- The level of branding and marketing built-in to the business (applies only to buying an existing business or franchise, or distributing a product not invented by you)

These variables will necessarily affect your business venture. Consider them carefully before proceeding. Do not be discouraged! Press on, because this is all worth the investment of time. Doing your homework can really pay off, as Rich-New writes that "74% of the wealthiest [Americans] are business owners." Be sure to have a solid *exit strategy*, however, as hiccups can occur.

Though her book is filled with cautionary tales, Rich-New ultimately falls in the same camp and myself and Kiyosaki. We all seem to agree that building your business is the surest way to become truly, lastingly wealthy.

Getting the Funding for Your Venture

You won't get very far without some initial (and, most likely, continuous) investment in your business. The amount of money you will need to get your operation off the ground will vary depending on the industry. You may be the primary contributor to your fledgling organization at first. If, however, your business model is sound and enticing, you might be able to get funding from family, friends or other individuals who might be interested in bankrolling you.

One of the greatest of Tranont's contributions to the American businessperson is its simplification of the funding issue. With a start-up cost of less than $500 and residual income, you could quickly find yourself solidifying your niche and expanding your business all while accruing money to reinvest into your assets.

ESTABLISHING CULTURE

Another aspect you should consider when starting your business is the feeling you most want it to embody. You have no doubt heard the phrase "corporate culture" used in reference to the nature of the work, people and office space of a particular business. Deciding on the "culture" you want for your own company is very important. Do you prefer to work in large teams or are you more of a do-it-yourselfer type? Would you rather always be engaging in very different kinds of activities, or do you enjoy focusing on a single kind of task? Consider, as well, your location. Would you want to work from a home office or rent an office space?

Now, get ready for some *very* exciting stuff.

THE COMPONENTS OF THE MOST SUCCESSFUL BUSINESSES

Though you only *need* to master a majority of the items on this list, the *most* successful businesses exemplify all of the following traits. A great business:

- Seizes the moment at the exact right time
- Exploits favorable market trends

- Offers *consumable* products or services that require repeat purchases
- Retains customers, rather than constantly relying on acquiring new ones
- Patents unique products and technological developments
- Develops strong compensation plans and wide profit margins
- Forms mutually-beneficial partnerships

Only the unwise underestimate the power of building a niche for your business. On the other hand, there are products and services that will likely never go out of style. You might build your business with the "liquor and lipstick" syndrome in mind, thus positioning yourself as a *counter-cyclical* enterprise. Don't be alarmed by that term, by the way. "Counter-cyclical" means only that, in a down economy, your business is still profitable. The reason for this is simple enough: even during a recession, most folks will still somehow find it within their means to buy those products that cater to their short-term pleasure response.

Pizza Hut is a great example of a counter-cyclical business that has done phenomenally well. In down times, people often turn to pizza as a cheap meal, using leftovers for days. When the economy is up, people order more pizza for parties and gatherings. Am I saying that you have to become as big as the nation's biggest pizza chain in order to own a viable business? Of course not. The point is that there are those products and services out there that folks simply can't seem to do without, no matter how much their wallets and purses are hurting at the time.

PROFIT PROJECTIONS AND POWERFUL PARTNERSHIPS

When starting a business, you will need to find a way to measure your profits in a way that makes sense. With Tranont as your ally, you will have access to the best tools currently available. We will be talking about that more in the next chapter.

Every great entrepreneur agrees that forming strong partnerships is the optimum way to ensure the success of your business. A word to the wise on that subject: take care in whom you invite into the fold. It is often better to *become* friends with the talent you bring in to work for you, rather than transforming friends into enemies due to a dispute. Both parties may mean well, but if your friend or acquaintance is not the absolute best fit for the job, you would be much better off hiring someone else.

Tranont, of course, makes the creation of partnerships easier and even more valuable to you and your business. As stated above, every time you, or someone you brought in, recruits a new associate, everyone takes home that much more money.

THE TWO KINDS OF START-UP

There are, fundamentally, only two kinds of businesses: those that *duplicate* and those that *innovate*. A duplication-oriented business focuses on providing a service or creating a product that already exists, but does a better job of it. An innovating business leverages creativity, plus time, plus determination to implement an idea that will solve a problem. This is also known as identifying a consumer's "point of pain." By offering a solution to that stress, the innovating company earns the custom.

MAKE A CHECKLIST

As you build your business, you might create a checklist, a working plan that you can change at any time. But this plan can guide you as you undertake the steps in the creative process. Here's an example that may prove useful to you:

- Develop the idea of your product (find the "point of pain" and create a solution)
- Identify your target audience, tailoring your marketing approach to their tastes
- Home in on the strongest benefits of your product or service
- Determine how best to fulfill your obligations to buyers (brick-and-mortar shop, digital store, etc.)
- As you become more stable, brainstorm ways to expand the reach of your business (mobile apps, licensing, etc.) — which Tranont makes easy for you
- Constantly revisit where you should spend more of your time, finding time for new training, informational webinars, etc.

THE TRUTH ABOUT STARTING A SUCCESSFUL BUSINESS

As you press on, remember these words. Use these to encourage yourself to never give up on your dream.

1. *If you don't sell, you don't earn:* your great product or service will amount to nothing unless you make the sale, so get out there!
2. *Always work to become wiser:* pursue learning opportunities wherever and whenever they arise.
3. *No runaway success was built overnight:* creating a business is not like brewing a pot of instant coffee.

Never fear experimentation. Always keep striving! Know that the number one cause for 80 percent of new business failures is a lack of funding. You will not suffer from that problem if you work with Tranont, so you have a tremendous advantage over your peers and competitors.

WHEN YOU ARE READY TO GO BUY A BUSINESS

If you feel your industry requires you keep an attorney on retainer, you should be prepared to pay top dollar. One of the biggest and most common blunders a new business owner can make is skimping on the legal aspect of running a company. There may come a day when you will be brought to court, justly or unjustly. At that time, you will want excellent legal representation. Fortunately, by that point, you will have learned how to effectively manage your business, in great part due to those detailed lessons courtesy of Tranont.

Additionally, when you are buying an existing business, good legal counsel can be of great use to you. The same goes for an excellent banker or CPA. Leaning on these professionals will give you the ability to perform your due diligence on any company you are looking to acquire. A smart lawyer could save you from buying a lemon, which would save you thousands (and potentially millions) in the long run.

Buying a business can seem inherently less risky than starting one fresh. After all, the results of profit projections are made more reliable when you have several years of previous data by which to measure the potential future. However, who can realistically predict macrocosmic economic trends? At least when you start a business, you know it from the inside out. You have been with it through every step of its growth.

You might also rightly suggest than an existing business has a built-in client base. That is true, but this could change with the tide. A shift in management can affect every aspect of the company in question.

When evaluating a business or franchise for potential acquisition, consider the following attributes:

- Is the infrastructure strong? How many employees?
- How many clients?
- What is the outlook for this industry five years from now? Ten years from now?

- Is the cash flow attractive? (Rich-New cites the statistic "that 90 percent of resale businesses with cash flow greater than $100,000 will still be operating more than five years after the sale") When you buy a business, its cash should immediately flow into your coffers. If that is not the case, you might reconsider your investment
- Does it qualify for a Small Business Administration (SBA) loan?
- Is the Return on Investment (ROI) healthy? What about the Return on Invested Capital (ROIC)?
- Did the seller seem desperate?

Take nothing at face value. Review all tax returns and other IRS records when assessing the business's financial picture. Beware of owners who attempt to hide anything at all from you.

BUYING A FRANCHISE

Franchising has its advantages. Here are a few of them:

- Big branding means wide-ranging name recognition
- Firmly established operations may require little input from you
- Training, customer support and recruitment processes are standardized
- Typically higher rates of success and lower inventory costs, due to corporate backing

The same questions listed in the previous section apply the process of purchasing a franchise. Be warned, franchising does come with some risks, namely:

- Initial investment may be steep
- There are lackluster or downright shady franchises out there
- You are not in control, your franchisor sets the rules
- Despite the advantages listed above, franchises still fail quite often

No matter the business structure in which you are thinking of investing, it is absolutely critical that you thoroughly investigate every angle before you make any decisions.

GETTING INTO NETWORK MARKETING

Of the approximately $141 billion in revenue generated by the network marketing industry's nearly 88 million salespeople, $28 billion is made within the United States. This business model of contracting individuals to sell products directly to clients is no novelty. Thus, it can be tempting to enter the fast-paced world of network marketing (which goes by several other names). Before you dive in head-first, however, there are a few details you should know:

- At entry level, your title will usually be "distributor," "independent distributer" or something along these lines.
- Depending on your position along the chain of command, you will be beholden to an "up-line" to the distributor who signed you up. In turn, "down-line," are distributors whom you bring in who will be beholden to you. Up-liners are coaches, providing training to those who are down-line.
- There are other terms with which you should familiarize yourself, such as "cross-line," "sponsor," "direct sales" and "end-user." Rich-New's book is an excellent source for industry-specific definitions and other information.
- When receiving commissions on regularly renewed products and services, you stand to earn significant *residual income* from this type of business, depending on the nature of that which you end up selling.

Network marketing businesses, when well-run, have distinct advantages. A few examples of these include:

- Name recognition, as with franchising

- Solid, established distribution, tracking and customer service practices
- In-house training
- Easy entry and limited risk due to the initial required investment typically being rather low
- Clear metrics for success; how well you do is tied to how much you sell

But there are some disadvantages:

- Easy come, easy go; because you as the business owner are not financially bound to the operation, you can drop out without incurring too much damage
- The particular kind of energy required to become a successful network marketer does not come naturally to everyone
- New network marketing companies are just as susceptible to failure as other business models
- A company offering only one or two products or services is less likely to withstand lean times

The way you oversee your business will depend on your focus. If "bottom-up," you will primarily be interacting directly with clients. A "top-down" means you will be recruiting others to do most, if not all, of the selling on your behalf. Reflecting on the effort necessary to train and educate recruits, the latter option can be time-consuming. Tranont, however, makes it easy, given its focus on providing to each of its associates the best tools and in-depth, but easy to comprehend, lessons.

THE MISSION AND VISION OF TRANONT

Tranont is here to support you, rain or shine. You can protect yourself against potential failures and, should you experience a setback, Tranont's national network is here to help you mitigate your losses.

That way, you can stay free to experiment and explore, refining your unique business proposition and processes. With a world-class suite of tools and a desire to see you develop the knowledge and skills that will enable you to succeed by your own steam, Tranont offers the best of financial education and training to foster wealth-building.

Tranont's mission, in a nutshell, is to change the world's economy, one household at a time. With such a strong and reliable umbrella over your head, even should the sky fall, you will be safe and secure. Work from home, from a rented office space or anywhere else. The overarching goal of Tranont's aggressive national expansion has been, and will continue to be, to create an environment within which you can build your own version of the New American Dream.

All Tranont associates are endowed with exceptional interpersonal communication skills, a tremendous talent for leadership, a great work ethic and, of course, the desire and motivation to achieve true financial freedom. If these qualities are important to you, too, you will likely fit right in.

The most powerful consumer direct marketing company ever conceived, network marketing has been hailed, including by financial masterminds like Warren Buffett, as a herald of the greatest shift in wealth of all time. With your help, we can bring about the rebirth of the American Dream.

In the next chapter, you will find a detailed description of the products that will help you over the course of your journey to true financial independence.

4 ·
THE PRODUCTS TO SHAPE
THE FUTURE

In the previous chapters, we discovered what has befallen this nation to cause the decay of what I call the Old American Dream. In addition, we found out why it is possible to create something better, salvaging a brighter future from the wreckage of the past. In Chapter 3, we saw *why* it was possible for you, the hard-working American citizen, to achieve complete financial independence. This current chapter will concern itself with *how* it is possible for you to amass enough wealth to embody the New American Dream.

Tranont has kindly made available a slew of solutions and products to all of its associates, streamlining the process of starting a business and ensuring you need never venture out into the wildernesses of local, national and international markets on your own.

MONEY TROUBLES

Those who do not stress about money on a daily basis represent a fortunate few. They are not the norm, but you can most definitely join their ranks. Are you concerned about your credit score, investments, retirement fund, mortgage payments and so on? Finding ways to save for your future and the future of your children can be made vastly more difficult by having to fret over how to scrape together enough money for the next car payment or trip to the grocery store. Loans, expenses, college educations, these can each cripple you, on their own. Together, they can keep you from getting out of bed in the morning, I know.

Maybe your financial situation was thrown for a loop when your identity was stolen or you were the victim of credit fraud. Do you feel the sensitive information you store online is currently secure? Tranont asks the question, do we have a nationwide, or even worldwide, financial problem?

An article on CNN Money reports that 31 percent of Americans have no retirement savings to their names. You know this already from personal experience, but it is obvious that the tax scene has been tough in America lately. An individual whose average income is $43,460 per year will pay $355,366 in taxes over the course of a 40 year career. That is no insignificant amount of money, to be sure. Forbes tells us that 401(k)s have failed America and that the majority of Americans will be forced to work well beyond the traditional age of retirement.

As if these facts did not paint a bleak enough picture of our nation's incredibly poor financial health, according to Reuters, Cyber crime is responsible for $445 billion in yearly losses. Your identity and, thus, your livelihood can be borrowed or outright stolen without you knowing until it is far too late.

There are many terrible statistics I could cite, but I can tell you nothing that common sense, your own experience, a cursory Google search or watching the news any day of the week could show you. It is no secret that we are in trouble, as individuals and as a nation.

BUT THERE IS ALWAYS HOPE

In response to the dire financial straits in which the majority of us find ourselves, Tranont put together a selection of products with the intent to fight as our champion. To combat all of the problems listed above, this company has focused on entrepreneurial education. As a result, thousands of success stories were born.

THERE IS WORK TO BE DONE

The task at hand is certainly not easy. A good deal of valor will be required. Looking at a hypothetical group of 100 people who have reached the age of 65, we behold a sobering breakdown. The Social Security Administration and Bureau of the Census tell us that 16 of these 100 will be dead before or by the time that they reach that age, while 66 will be forced to survive on less than $30,000 per year, 13 will lay claim to incomes greater than $30,000 and 5 will have more than $60,000. Only 1 percent of Americans will actually be wealthy by the time they reach age 65.

BREAKING DOWN THAT FIRST PERCENTILE

Splitting apart that top 1 percent, we see that it is comprised of athletes and entertainers. Unfortunately, most of us cannot hope to join the ranks of pop stars, award winning actors, singers, guitarists, quarterbacks and the Kobe Bryants of this world. A more realistic solution is necessary.

Moving down the list, we see that sales associates make up another 5 percent of this bracket of the wealthiest Americans. Top professionals encompass another 10 percent, as do CEOs and those who invest in the Stock Market. What if you are not a salesperson? How does one become a "top professional," you ask? Maybe you don't know the first thing about stocks.

Not to worry! There is some good news on the way. We have not taken a close look at the remaining 74 percent, after all. Well, this group of wealthy, successful people is entirely populated by business owners. Entrepreneurs make up the bulk of the richest Americans!

The American Entrepreneurial Spirit is Why Tranont Exists

Tranont was formed with the mission in mind to help you uplift yourself and join the ranks of that 74 percent. That is why Tranont has maintained a strong focus on the financial services industry, which is one of the world's largest, generating over $3 trillion in revenue and representing nearly 8 percent of the United States' Gross Domestic Product (GDP).

To bring about the sweeping changes required, Tranont formed a series of strategic partnerships with major companies like Chase, Visa, US Bank, Master Card, Merrill Lynch, Wells Fargo, Bank of America, American Express, ING, Citibank, Discover, HSBC and so on.

Impact Your Life Financially

How many of us can say we were taught anything truly useful about money in school? Because our parents received little better in the way of a financial education, we could not have gotten much from them. Tranont saw this less-than-ideal situation and found a way to address it: an online and live curriculum designed to teach you everything you need to know to take control of your financial destiny.

How would you assess the quality of the financial education you received over your lifetime thus far? More importantly, would you consider yourself *financially literate*? Don't worry if the answer is "no." No one is here to point fingers or cast aspersions, because so many have found and will continue to find themselves in your shoes.

> **"Luck is what happens when preparation meets opportunity."**
>
> *- Seneca*

But what will you do from here? Will you seize the opportunity lying before you? Will you take that road less traveled, that right fork in the path of life? Tranont offers its hand in guidance for whenever you are ready to reach out and take it. The classes available to you range in complexity, starting with the basics: *Financial Literacy 101,* if you will. When contrasted with the steep tuition of the "school of hard-knocks," this deal seems a no-brainer.

Before you can learn the basics, or further your skills if you already have reached or exceeded a basic understanding of the world of finance, it would be expedient to be able to access all the pertinent information in one place, wouldn't you agree? That's where this first core product comes into play.

Core Product: Tranont OneView

Today's turbulent financial landscape puts many average Americans at a disadvantage that can seem like an insurmountable obstacle. Even if you make a herculean effort to educate yourself about the ins and outs of this lightning-paced world, in which numbers, charts and graphs flit by like bats out of hell, it can still feel stifling and daunting to manage your investments and savings. There are so many financial sites to keep track of, so many documents needing to be cataloged. The prodigious nature of this process has left a great deal of folks disoriented and confused.

In answer, Tranont OneView provides a handy and intuitive way to reassemble all those disparate pieces of the puzzle, keeping them straight. Fully integrated with 16,000 financial institutions nationwide, this product gives you an instant and comprehensive overview of all of your finances. Additionally, you will have at your fingertips the power to quickly create spending plans and budgets. With real-time transaction updates, financial alerts and news about ripples in the wider financial waters, you will stay abreast of both your personal accounts and the latest important information. Through your tablet or Smartphone, set and track financial goals from anywhere. Receive email notifications on the go, along with personal advice tailored to your objectives.

Tranont OneView is your one-stop access point to everything you need to track, whenever you need to track it. Some accounts may only need a one-over every week or two, while others might require daily checkups. With Tranont OneView, you will never have to worry about which is which, or which password goes with what account. Find it all in one convenient place.

Do you worry about your online security? If you do, that's very wise of you. Considering you now have money management tools, spending and budgeting plans and every other component of your total financial picture in one place, you will want to be sure your sensitive information is completely secure. That is why Tranont allied itself with the biggest names in online security, including VeriSign, McAfee and Truste, to provide the maximum level of protection currently possible. The days of worrying about identity theft, viruses, spyware, malware and other online threats are over. As an added layer of defense, Tranont OneView *will never store* any information about you or your accounts, up to and including your balance. You own these, and thus you are the only one who can edit or change any details concerning your accounts.

All associates are given access to Tranont OneView, a web-based software application that joins all of your scattered checking, savings and investment accounts all around the globe into one conveniently accessed location.

There are several other ways in which Tranont's Cloud protects you.

CORE PRODUCT: TRANONT DEFEND

Tranont has partnered with Invisus to defend your security, identity, privacy and finances against any and all threats resultant from the advent of this new, digital age. With Tranont and Invisus on your side, you could imagine your accounts as a Welsh medieval castle. Hackers and other hooligans, in this daydream, are the barbarians at the gates. You can sit safely in your tower, listening to Tranont and Invisus, your valiant knight commanders, dumping hot oil and tar down on any who would try to enter your domain without your express permission.

The Internet is a wonderful tool for connecting with family, friends and acquaintances the world over. At the click of a button or the swipe of a finger, you can track your favorite stocks, pay your bills, order Chinese food and read or watch national and international news. Yet, hand-in-hand with these amazing technological bounds, cyber crime is always on the rise. Just as you would not know the day without the night, the height of our interconnectivity drags in within it a host of undesirables.

Tens of millions of people fall victim to identity theft and many other cyber crimes each and every year. Hackers work tirelessly and around the clock to steal your money, ruin your credit or commit fraud using your good name, dragging your digital reputation through the mud. Their shameless and depraved activities can cause you a great deal of stress and headaches, but, more seriously, such attacks could result in your complete financial ruin.

Whether or not you will be accosted by these vile individuals is not so much a question of "if" but "when." Nearly all of us have been or will be caught at one point or another, and we may not even have known it was happening at the time. Last year alone, there were over ten million cases of identity theft, according to CBS DC. There are many species of viruses out there that demand constant vigilance.

One powerful example is the Gameover Zeus Trojan virus, also called ZeuS or Zeus bot. Up to one million computers have been infected by this virus since 2011, causing $100 million dollars in losses, as reported by CNN Money. And that's only counting victims in the U.S. Zeus spread its influence, linking a vast network of chained computers, targeting thousands of small businesses across the country.

In tandem with Cryptolocker, a program that encrypts a computers files, Zeus held the sensitive financial and personal information of millions hostage in exchange for ransom.

Viruses like this one, along with malware, adware, spyware and so on, grant the more nefarious elements of society access to banking and other private information. In the last 12 months, millions upon millions of folks have had their personal information stolen due to data breaches at businesses, medical offices, insurance companies, universities and government databases.

Tranont Defend answers the call to arms, rising to the challenge of blocking and preempting any threats to your financial safety. A full suite of expert products and services protect your identity, security and finances against the disastrous characteristic of the digital age.

To begin with, *Tranont Defend Elite Personal* stops at the door those looking to steal your identity through credit monitoring and reporting. Ensure your computer is working at optimum efficiency from here on out with *Extreme PC Makeover*, a full, one-time computer tune-up and security checkup. You will also have a problem repair service on standby, giving you that highly desirable peace of mind. *iCare PC* gives you unlimited computer tech support and computer security service. Joining the *Cyberhood Watch* folds you into a community of users protected by internet safety alerts and who are given a wide array educational resources.

Financial and identity safeguards must be inextricably bound, which is Tranont Defend applies itself to strengthening the walls of your digital castle against any would-be invaders. It guards all of your many portals of access, including iPads, PCs, laptops and more. These services, together, keep you safe and securely on the track towards wealth. Stop nefarious ne'er-do-wells who could swoop in and destroy all that you have worked so hard to build at the gates, before they can do any damage. Without the burdens of concerning yourself over hackers and other online dangers, you will have more time to transform your dream into a reality.

Core Product: Tranont Tax

You might work hard for decades, putting your back into it day in and day out for what can seem like an eternity. As the years stretch, you could very well end up finding that you are making little to no headway. Worse, despite your best efforts, you might even be backsliding. How frustrating is it to realize that, no matter how much blood, sweat and tears you invest in your career, you are trotting in place? Many of us have been, or still are, there. We know one of the biggest and most egregious culprits in depriving us of our hard earned coin is the tax man. But we should also remember the Parable of Minas, Matthew 25:14-30, whose lesson can be summed up quite neatly: you should work with what you have to multiply your wealth.

In this parable, a master divided among his three servants eight talents. Five went to one, two to another and one to the last. The first two went out trading. He who was given five talents not only brought these back to his master but also earned five talents in addition to the initial amount. The servant who received two talents also doubled his portion of his master's wealth. The third servant buried the talent in the dirt, where it could do neither good nor ill, which made the master cross once he heard what his servant had done (or failed to do, rather). The moral of the story is that, regardless of what you start with, you should always be seeking to better your position. If your only talent is fearfully burying talents, you will have no time to develop those talents you need to earn more talents.

The Parable of Minas applies in two ways to what we are discussing in this section. Firstly, vast amounts of wealth are lost each year to the tax man, who is adept at *digging up* talents from the dirt. Therefore, fear is not useful in this case. Secondly, these lost talents cannot be reinvested by you, preventing you from making any headway on the road to financial freedom.

This sorry state of affairs can be put behind you. *Tranont Tax* gives you tools to legally save as much money as you can on your taxes. When that fateful day rolls around the bend again, you can look Uncle Sam right in the eye, having paid your fair share and, for once, *no more.*

How does it work? Take business expenses as an example. These can quickly get out of control if you do not have the right tracking system in place. You have no hope of maximizing your refund without a system tallying all those costs of doing business. Fortunately, tracking and managing expenses has been made much simpler. Even mileage can be accurately represented thanks your mobile device, and with a little help from Tranont. Its cutting-edge app integrates with your Smartphone's GPS, logging your routes automatically. Forget about having to rely on calculating mileage by odometer reading, relying mostly on guesswork come tax day. The app will serve like a personal assistant, giving you the most accurate representation, day by day, of how much you will be able to save by deducting your mileage. Tranont Tax keeps other running tallies through its real-time deductibles tracking service.

You can also attached photos of receipts or other documents. With automatic tracking, GPS integration, and a host of other features that are all compatible with PCs, laptops, tablets and Smartphones, Tranont Tax can really simplify any potential future audits. The best part is that this service is one of many included with a Tranont associate's basic monthly fee.

TRANONT EDUCATION

As previously mentioned, an integral facet of Tranont's altruistic mission is to educate you and hopefully inspire you with tips and advice geared toward starting and running your own business. These video lessons are presented in the style of a lecture and feature many expert speakers. You will be learning from folks who were in your position not too long ago. They worked their way up and became the heroes or heroines of their very own shining success stories.

The topics range in complexity from the very basics, like the definition of inflation, to much more intricate subjects. Samples of these lessons can be found on www.TeamworldMarketing.com as well as YouTube. The full videos are made available to Tranont associates, as are an assortment of informative webinars. Featured speakers include our friend, Ron Glover, and many other wise and wealthy business owners.

Simply put, *Tranont Education* encompasses a set of on-demand financial and personal development classes. The aim is to educate each associate (meaning you, the business owner) to enable you to better understand the technical details tied up with managing your finances. The other side of that goal is to inspire you while providing you with the tools to change your financial situation, and thus change your life.

Aside from these core products, Tranont has more ways for you to streamline your journey to wealth.

Business to Business and Communications Products

These days, fewer and fewer people tolerate a business that does not accept major credit cards. If you only deal in cash or checks, you are missing out. Don't worry, though, because Tranont can get you in the game. In partnership with National Processing, you will receive the guaranteed lowest rates for *credit card processing services*. Screening solutions are also available to you any time you feel these are necessary to lend you peace of mind. *Background checks* take up to 36 hours to come back to you. Also remember that, just for setting up this account, you will be earning *residual income*.

Remain connected to your partners, your colleagues and your subordinates through the most reliable cell phone service around. Tranont has already joined forces with Verizon and will soon add AT&T and T-Mobile to its list of allies. With Voice over Internet

Protocol (VOIP) business phone services and unparalleled cell phone coverage, Tranont keeps you in touch with everyone in your extended circles.

LICENSED PRODUCTS: TRANONT LIFE, LLC.

Aside from protection, education and interconnectivity, Tranont also provides you with the best insurance and investment products. Though requiring a licensing fee, once you have added these to your arsenal, you will earn yet another stream of income. Even should you choose to forgo these licensed opportunities, through Tranont you can still generate a *substantial* second income. In fact, as we saw in the previous chapter, once you really get going with those referrals, running your business with Tranont as your partner could transform this venture into your *primary* source of income. That is the power of *residual income*, the results of which can rapidly compound and take you from rags to riches.

But why should you invest in Tranont Life, you ask? There are many reasons, the first and foremost of which is the safety of your family. There may come a day, as you grow your business, that you will butt heads with an ornery customer or another litigious party. The crook's "get rich quick" scheme is to sue legitimate business owners in order to snatch a "piece of the action." If your business faces a drawn-out lawsuit, you and your family could potentially lose everything you have worked so hard to build. Not to mention that any damage done to your reputation takes a long, long time to repair. Shield your family from disaster by separating, through Tranont Life, your private life from your public one.

Other benefits include tax-deferred growth of your retirement fund and tax-free withdrawals. Why should you pay taxes on the same lump sum year after year after year? You should be able to pay your fair share once and be done with it. Thereafter, any time you want to access your money, you should not be subjected to additional taxes and fees that will cost you big over time. Tranont Life gives you the means to manage your investments while minimizing the costs associated with such tasks.

Finally, in Chapter 3 we determined how explosive index growth can be, especially when compared with the languid S&P 500. Investing in stocks requires a more active style of management than simply throwing your money at the 500 biggest companies in America and hoping things will turn out alright. Tranont Life's indexing tools are refined and meticulously managed. They represent a no-nonsense, low-maintenance way for you to exponentially increase your wealth long-term.

One video I found on YouTube featured a presentation by Lorne Berry, Founder and CEO of Tranont, explaining a little bit about Tranont Life. During his presentation, he talked about how there exist scant few resources out there for investors looking to significantly grow their asset portfolios. A Certificate of Depreciation (CD), for example, is stable and bears no downside. This stability, however, comes at the cost of pathetically weak growth. They are not necessarily a horrible investment, but if you cannot keep up with inflation, you are *losing money each year*. The other example Berry cited were death benefits, an amount of money paid to a beneficiary upon the death of the insured party. Of course, it is a good idea to buy a life insurance policy, but you don't want to ever need the boost in income resulting from a tragedy.

That's why Tranont Life is such a valuable addition to your treasure trove. We have already seen how powerful Tranont Life's indexing service can be, but let's review with this latest video in mind. Therein, Berry showed that the S&P 500, over the course of a 14 year term beginning in 2000, generated growth of 13, 23, 26 and even 29 percent. By all appearances, and depending on the year, it seemed you could do quite well. What about the other years in that period, though? They paint a very different picture. Negative growth as low as -10, -13,

-23 or -38 percent occurred sporadically throughout this time period. All in all, $100,000 invested in the year 2000 would become $126,995 by the year 2014. That figure seems decent at first glance, maybe. At least, it does until we see that, with Tranont Life, that same $100,000, by 2014, would have grown to $285,835. The difference in quality of result is obviously astronomical.

TRANONT LIFE BRINGS PEOPLE TOGETHER

To create powerful results, Tranont Life unites individuals, families and small business owners with some of the largest insurance companies and financial service providers in America. The goal is to rapidly change the lives of middle-income families. One of the top marketing organizations operating in the country, Tranont and Tranont Life's mission is to change the world's economy, one household at a time.

As I wrote about in the Introduction and first two chapters of this book, too many people feel overwhelmed by or trapped in their current financial situation. Tranont understands that its associates come from all walks of life, that they possess differing levels of financial education and preparedness. It is because of this empathic understanding that I have come to respect Tranont. This company really does offer up a series of great solutions in a time of multiplying problems.

Tranont has already helped so many Americans realize their dreams of achieving real and lasting wealth. The process of managing one's investments is made much less intimidating thanks to the principles and practices they teach and the tools they offer up. No matter your unique situation, Tranont almost certainly has something up its sleeve to suit your needs.

TAKE BACK CONTROL OF THE WHEEL

Do you feel your ship is headed straight for rocky waters? Tranont can help you take hold of the wheel and make that sharp turn before it's too late. Changing your heading is of greater necessity now than ever before, because pensions are no longer guaranteed, employer-matching of contributions to 401(k)s is dying out and generous government benefits increasingly the exception rather than the rule.

Life insurance and annuities will soon embed themselves as a fundamentally important part of any viable plan for financial stability. Due to the fact that we live in uncertain economic times, the time to act is *now*. Americans need to take action immediately to secure their futures.

> **Create a definite plan for carrying out your desire and begin at once, whether you ready or not, to put this plan into action.**
>
> *- Napoleon Hill*

Tranont Life is not interested in doing everything for you. You will have all the support you could ever want or ask for, but, in the end, you will be the one making the decisions that will shape your future. Would you have it any other way? I certainly would not. Rest assured that every decision you do make will be informed by the educational services provided by Tranont.

One of the ways by which you can prepare for your journey to wealth is by taking advantage of Tranont Life's Confidential Needs Analysis (CNA), a process which identifies your financial needs and goals so that you can make the wisest and most practicable choices going forward. A CNA will cost you nothing and you will be under no obligation to follow the advice given or purchase any additional services or products. You will meet with a licensed Tranont associate, during which time you will both evaluate your situation. Employing understandable language, rather than obscure jargon, the associate will share with you actionable tips and strategies.

A CNA gives you and your family the chance to assess your finances without the unneeded stress of a sales pitch. Be aware that the complimentary, hands-on CNA should not be considered a complete financial plan but rather a more generalized series of guidelines you can follow to shorten your hike to the top of the mountain. That being said, the combined experience of Tranont Life associates, bolstered by the company's extensive industry contacts, really does give the best chance to get a leg up in life.

Prepare for your future and save money for emergencies. And if tragedy should ever befall your family, you will give your loved ones the means to continue on, secure in their future. There are many varied options from which to make your selection. Find the best choice at www.TranontLife.net/life-insurance. A very few examples of the insurance and financial service providers represented are: Fidelity & Guaranty Life Insurance Company, American National Insurance Company and VOYA. Soon enough, you can quickly build a basic but very solid foundation from which to build your own version of the New American Dream.

CLOSING THIS CHAPTER

We have seen how devastated the American financial landscape has become. With so many people hurting, it can at times appear as if the rot has permanently set in, down to the last household. But Tranont numbers among those companies that are working to eliminate the damages done by debt and many of the other financial woes plaguing our society.

When you take out a loan, it is the interest that kills you slowly over time, if you let the payments get away from you. Imagine, for a moment, that you could take out a loan from yourself. You would then pay *yourself* the interest. Does that sound too far-fetched? Well, it shouldn't, because that is precisely what Tranont's *Smart Banking Strategies* can allow you to do. The average American loses so much wealth through payments, fees and mounting interest on loans. The cycle is a vicious one. In response, Tranont asks, *why not keep that wealth at home?*

The above is but one way in which Tranont is working to liberate America from debt, one household at a time. What if you could completely free yourself from the burdens of debt and constant worry about your finances? What if you could step outside your door and see that every home — to the left, to the right and across — had experienced the same dramatic change?

Tranont invites you to help change the world by changing the way you deal with your own money. There are many incentives, aside from the satisfaction of a job well-done, for joining this journey. The best of these has to be *residual income:* by simply passing on Tranont's positive message, you can *bring home money.* You profit when Tranont does, and vice versa.

If there is a surer, better way to bring about the New American dream, I have not yet found it, and I don't expect to any time soon. As we will continue to see throughout the remainder of this book, Tranont gives you the tools you need to accomplish all the steps listed in Chapter 2, from building your asset column to starting your business.

In the next chapter, we will be taking a look at some of the rising stars of Tranont, gaining valuable insights and inspiration as we move along.

5.

THE RISING STARS AND KEY PLAYERS OF TRANONT

In some respects, this chapter may well be the most important of all in this entire book. Keeping in mind the mission of Tranont, which is, in essence, to help Americans achieve financial freedom and build real wealth, we should take a moment to read and reflect on a series of success stories.

What makes these triumphs particularly spectacular is the fact that they are completely real and down to earth. The following stories are all centered on real Americans, like you and me, who made something of themselves. With help from Tranont, they saw what was and dreamed of what could be. But there was no magic involved! Dedication to one's personal success is the first ingredient. Sprinkle in some financial education, courtesy of Tranont, and a positive, can-do attitude, and you have yourself a recipe for lasting wealth.

> **"The greatest discovery of my generation is that human beings can alter their lives by altering their attitudes of mind."**
>
> *-William James*

As you will see, the New American Dream is not only within reach, it has been touched and latched onto by so many already. My hope for this chapter is that it will inspire you to take that initial leap of faith, to spread your wings and fly.

To that end, I present a selection of individuals who have grown with Tranont into powerful business owners and entrepreneurs. These are nothing as trite as "testimonials"; what you are about to read are true American success stories. You could be next.

JAKE SPENCER

Jake Spencer has been in the multilevel marketing and direct sales business for over 11 years. He was introduced to Tranont by Scott Bland, who is one of the company's founders, and a personal friend for many years. Currently, Spencer is the head consultant for Tranont. His long-term goal is to one day see the company compete on a global scale.

With such a wealth of experience at his command, Spencer may be ideally suited to dispel some myths about multilevel marketing: "obviously, the big misconception in MLM [sic] is people don't value it as a real business." He explains that, because the start up cost of an MLM business is "hundreds of dollars, not thousands," both owners and potential customers alike tend to undervalue the business. This often leads to lax management and lackluster advocacy for the products, which, in turn, lead to the decay of the business. Worse, any opportunity for real profit and wealth accrual is lost.

Spencer also laments the more common than not perception that MLM is a "get-rich-quick scheme." He strongly disagrees, stating that real success in the business is possible, but that it requires real work. People who get really rich really quickly are the exception, rather than the rule. "The rule," according to Spencer, is that people who put in "three, five, seven years of consistent, steady work — sometimes hard work" — can actually build real wealth over time.

Endowed with that timeless American spirit of industry, Spencer tells us that "Companies are built. They're built with great people." All you need is "the right mindset" and a penchant for curiosity. Oh, and the drive to do some hard work to better your own life. "You're going to have to refine yourself," he says. "You're going to have to have some personal growth. You're going to have to read some books." As we shall see in greater detail in Chapter 6, Spencer is right on the money.

Setting aside the raw earning potential of Tranont's licensed products, what really drew Spencer to the company was its philosophy. In his own words: "Hey, let's help someone make money. But let's also help them keep money, and let us protect them and… educate them…" For Spencer, the chance to make "real residual income," while giving others the opportunity to develop that same ability, is what gets him to jump out of bed in the morning.

The secret of who makes money and who does not is not-so-secret, after all. There is an abundance of money to be made in the financial planning arena. This fact has been common knowledge for decades. The most common deterrent, however, is accessibility. Most companies tend to cloak themselves in mystery, to discourage newcomers and customers alike by remaining entirely inscrutable. Tranont simplifies that mess by building upon a basic, but inherently very powerful philosophy: "put up good products in the right people's hands" and always maintain integrity. The next step is educating incoming associates. All of these factors combine to form a highly comprehensible and, thus, effective package. Stressing the accessibility of what Tranont has to offer, Spencer claims that MLM "gives the average person, like myself, a real, true opportunity to own a business at a very minimal cost and work at it part-time, [in one's] spare time." Eventually, one can "cut the string and have it actually be a career," as it has been for Spencer for well over a decade.

The value of Tranont is most easily discerned in the services it offers. The tools come with education, allowing an associate to use said tools far more efficiently than he or she might have otherwise done. The fact that the company actually "care[s] about the people that are getting involved" and showing them what they stand to earn over the next five to ten years, is phenomenal. Forget about disposable products that nobody needs. With Tranont, you will be selling highly valuable and highly valued services.

Spencer warns that, as far recruitment is concerned, Tranont is not interested in "anyone and everyone." What sets Tranont apart is its integrity. Spencer paraphrases the principle that lies at the heart of the company's very existence: "It's important to say what you mean and mean what you say." Giving back to employees, those whose labors built the companies affiliated with Tranont, and engaging in many charitable enterprises is all part and parcel of the daily operations of Tranont.

"The MLM world opens up doors and many relationships and that's what a lot of people don't understand... You're not out there looking for businesses. You're not out there looking for ventures. You're not out there looking for investments. You're actually out there looking to build a network, to build relationships with people because business deals come down to people. People buy people. They don't buy products. They don't buy businesses."

According to Spencer, "a void" has occupied a space at the heart of the MLM industry "for decades." Tranont's products filled this void, ascertaining that "a lot of high-level people [in the MLM industry], like myself," would take notice. He states that "it's not secret [sic] that getting involved in a good MLM with a strong comp plan gives you the opportunity to make a lot of money. I can say a lot because I've known people who have made a lot of money." The tax breaks alone give home businesses a huge advantage, making the money even more attractive than most people believe it to, at first.

And yet, the industry has existed in a state of pseudo-limbo for such a long time. Until, that is, Tranont steps in. Spencer admits, "I don't know if it really takes as much money as what people think to start businesses" provided "you're with the right people." Tranont gives us the tools and know-how to transform dreams into reality and drive the resultant startup business into the stratosphere.

Spencer's personal goal is to prove instrumental in the ascension of Tranont to the status of billion-dollar company. And he wants to see that result come about in fewer than three years. He reiterates his commitment to charitable enterprises, but stresses that the best thing he believes he can do is grow Tranont to epic proportions. An even stronger Tranont will enable it to employ more and more people, benefiting even more families across the nation. Tranont has already infused money into so many local economies, Spencer sees no reason why it could not do the same on a global scale. "My goal is to really spearhead the expansion of what Tranont is doing," he states. "We want to take it to a billion dollars. We want to be a household name and we want to have tens of thousands of people benefiting from not just the customer source, great services [and] products, but also the associates that I work with."

HOW TRANONT HAS RAPIDLY CHANGED THE LIFE OF JAKE SPENCER

The biggest difference Tranont has brought to Spencer's life is that "it has gotten me excited again." A seasoned veteran in the MLM industry, he is excited to build something worthwhile, to see the looks on people's faces when they realize they are simultaneously paying off their debts and, finally, increasing their wealth. That's the whole point: funneling extra income into American households every month, while allowing these business owners to educate themselves on terminology and practices integral to success in the financial industry. Tranont is able to show its associates how they "could have been ahead with the same amount of money that they're already making," had they been properly educated. For Spencer, it's never too late to change a life. He is proud to be with Tranont, to give so many deserving individuals a second chance and a new lease on life.

He calls his experiences with Tranont, thus far, "awesome." It's about the success of the people. Obviously, our associates first, [as well as] our customers." One of the pleasures Spencer derives from life is receiving texts, phone calls and emails thanking him, and Tranont, for all they have done. Still, Spencer keeps himself humble. "I'm not looking for thank-yous," he says. He just wants as many people as possible to be given the opportunity he has, to "make a lot of money and change [one's] life."

Ron Glover

Ron Glover cut his teeth in the direct sales and network marketing industries and has over thirty years of experience in those fields. He is much more than a financial guru; he is practically a force of nature. Ever since a friend introduced him to Tranont on October 19, 2013, he has been fully committed to ensuring the rise of that company to the highest heights of the financial world.

Glover believes that Tranont could easily become the "number one financial services company in the nation" within the next five years, which is why he was so excited to get in on the ground floor of such a "dynamic" company. In fact, he left a very lucrative position in a strong, wide-reach organization in order to fully devote himself to building up the edifice that is Tranont.

> "[With Tranont,] I can see a tremendous opportunity to make money and to help other people. Selling products and services to people that they already use, such as life insurance, merchant processing, et cetera, you know?... I can see a company put a suite of products together that I didn't have to convince people to use because they already use them and already need them. So I call it 're-directional spending' — where you take money and spend it in better areas."

One of the reasons that Glover so resolutely advocates that everyone and anyone join with Tranont is its history. There is no better way to hitch one's wagon to a shooting star than to sign up with this offshoot of a massive company, MMR Direct, that is "almost 20 years old [and] that's done almost $2 billion in sales."

Over the course of his 38 years in the business, not once has Glover seen anything like Tranont. Due to its formula of mixing direct sales, teambuilding and network marketing into one homogenous whole, the company is poised to create the greatest and most successful industry in the financial services world. "I think this opportunity is second to none," Glover asserts, adding that, with Tranont unleashing the dormant potential of life insurance contracts, Americans can make "100 times more money" than with any other company, MLM or otherwise.

When asked what he sees himself doing over the next handful of years, Glover proclaims, "I plan on helping launch Tranont around the nation. I plan... to be traveling into different major cities and help[ing open] the markets as a leader with Tranont. So I feel like what I'm going to be doing is spending a lot of personal time helping launch new markets... In Denver, Dallas, Boston, San Diego, Chicago, Florida, Houston, all through California."

Personally, Glover thinks he could set up a residual income of $1 million per month within the next three years by building an organization in excess of 10 or 20,000 folks. However, the most important thing, he reminds us, is to "make a major impact in the lives of thousands of other people in the financial arena. Not only with our products that we have currently, but with our financial tools and education." In short, "We're going to teach people how to protect, manage, invest, save and make more money."

HOW TRANONT HAS RAPIDLY CHANGED THE LIFE OF RON GLOVER

At the age of 57, Glover is looking to the future. Currently single, thanks to Tranont, he can pour all of his energies into his daughter's success. He has already involved her daughter with in his business, guiding her down the path of true financial freedom (and paying off her first car in the process!). Essentially, what Glover and his daughter are doing is building a future filled with hope for themselves, each other, their family and anyone else whose lives they might touch.

By being able to build a business on "a very solid and firm foundation with legendary leadership," Glover has reevaluated his retirement, believing he can now personally do better while, at the same time, changing the lives of friends, neighbors and fellow Americans across the country. He lauds the incredible and highly "ethical management team" that made Tranont a reality that is truly accessible to average Americans. Building real, lasting wealth has never been more within reach.

JOHN BERGQUIST

With over 15 years in the financial services industry, John Bergquist has become one of the top leaders within the Tranont organization and has done so at a rapid pace. John was introduced to Tranont through Bill Ray and Scott Webb, who were friends of Mr. Bergquist and had worked closely with him in his former company. According to Bergquist, there were two major reasons that convinced him to join Tranont; the first being: "non-licensed products that could help people make money and start to build residual income while they were getting licensed." This was something his former company lacked to provide to its associates which led to a low retention rate. Because Tranont provides a direct sales avenue along with its licensed products, new associates can hit the ground running and earn while they learn the financial side of the company. The second reason for Bergquist's decision to join Tranont: ownership. The acquisition bonus which would eventually come to those who helped build Tranont to a billion dollar company convinced Bergquist to build his business here instead of anywhere else. He states: "the ability to own part of Tranont in that way" made Tranont a unique opportunity he could not let slip away.

When asked elaborate on what makes Tranont unique, Bergquist states: "there isn't anybody else who's doing things the same". In his eyes, Tranont stands out from all other MLM opportunities in that it has the ability to "pull the masses into the company through a word-of-mouth-approach by referring instead of selling Tranont's licensed and non-licensed products". Tranont also "allows people to grow their business and financial literacy very quickly" because of the financial plan they receive upon joining Tranont. Bergquist says "The ability to help people in this all-important area of finance definitely attracted me to be here, to stay here, and to grow here, and has given me the satisfaction and fulfillment to do so with all of those I've been able to help along the way".

For those looking at Tranont for the first time, Bergquist exhorts them to "have an open mind and see what we can do for them." He urges them to "see how we can help them with their financial plan." Whether that's making money, saving money on the services they're already spending money on, or whether that's looking at Tranont's investment plans that help people build, manage, protect, save, and invest their money wisely, Tranont has the resources they need to do it."

Berguist sees Tranont dominating the marketplace in the near future through its philosophy of helping one home at a time establish and commit to a financial plan. When it comes to investing, people usually make poor decisions, mostly because of the ignorance and inexperience in knowing where to put it and how to properly diversify. With Tranont, he looks forward to "truly delivering for Middle America and helping them establish plans that are predictable and sustainable so that Americans can truly have a chance to not only hit their goals, but exceed them with right work ethic." In the next five years, he sees Tranont spreading throughout the U.S. and eventually going global with an increased presence in the financial arena. Bergquist goes on to emphasize that: "Tranont allows Americans to have the right tools and products, along with the proper financial education to help them build real wealth and overcome the huge problem throughout the nation of not being able to retire financially independent. Personally, Bergquist sees himself "totally and completely financially free", something that such a small percentage of Americans can actually say. He also sees himself helping Tranont become, in terms of reps, the largest financial services company in the world.

How Tranont has Rapidly Changed the Life of John Bergquist

"The ability to help people in this all-important area of finance definitely attracted me to be here, to stay here, and to grow here, and has given me the satisfaction and fulfillment to do so with all of those I've been able to help along the way".

In 2015, John Bergquist was awarded with The Top VP promotion setting a record in the month of May for recruiting and financial planning. "Tranont has allowed me to grow and build a lot quicker than I was before, and therefore, be able to train, teach, and coach many others at a bigger and faster scale than I had been able to do before". Bergquist also credits Tranont for having him expand his personal development in ways he didn't think he could reach in order to achieve Tranont's big goals and the company's mission statement of making a huge difference in the communities and the economies we live in. "Through the help and mentorship from Tranont's leaders, Lorne Berry, Scott Bland, and Jake Spencer, I've been able to expand and grow exceedingly fast; faster than I have been to before." In summation, through Tranont's unique opportunity, its products and services, its leaders, and its inspiring philosophy, John Bergquist has been able to revitalize his career and has allowed him to change the outlook of his own life and the life and future of those he serves along the way.

CINDY FARFAN

Cindy Farfan has always been an entrepreneur. From a very young age, she took it upon herself to provide products and services that served the needs of those around her. There has never been a time in which she was not running one business or another, including auto dealerships, restaurants, a communication satellite company and so on. In her own words: "I guess you could say I've [always] been an entrepreneur at heart." She appreciates the fact that, through Tranont, she has since developed a strong foundation in finances which has greatly benefitted her overall business acumen.

Farfan has been with Tranont since late 2013, keeping herself so busy that the passing months have all become "a blur." To her, as with so many others, the time spent is less important than the manner in which she, consistently and on a daily basis, is driving her own success. When you love what you do, she would be the first to tell you, it hardly seems like work.

Having learned and grown under the protective umbrella of Tranont, Farfan now specializes in finances, an area which differs significantly from her previous experiences. The financial education that Tranont offers is just one of many services that bring value to individuals and communities across the nation. Farfan acknowledges how, thanks to the company's initiatives, anyone who joins the cause can see great results and amass savings. That capital can then be reallocated according to *your* designs and desires.

Acquiring new skills is only one small part of the value her business has imparted upon her life. Farfan explains, "What I love about Tranont is that we don't fill up people's garages with things they can't consume fast enough [and] end up having to give away."

"You get to own a piece of Tranont. That's one of the biggest reasons why I joined Tranont, because the opportunity is equal to everyone. We all have the same possibility of success and owning a business…"

Farfan revels in the joys of owning her own business and, thus, being able to set her own hours. As a result, she has been able to maximize her potential in both the career and personal sides of her life. The future looks brighter still, according to her own positive outlook: "I see myself as a million dollar earner with the company, having one of the biggest organizations and being very well-known within."

Of course, in line with the spirit of Tranont, Farfan's own personal and professional growth also serves the noble purpose of uplifting those around her. She desires nothing more than to help her family, friends and neighbors succeed as she did.

Farfan deems Tranont's future to be very bright, indeed. "I see our services being taken globally." As the company grows, and more spectacular products are added along the way, there is no telling how grand and sweeping the New American Dream could become. Farfan simply states, "I expect their growth to be gigantic."

How Tranont has Rapidly Changed the Life of Cindy Farfan

Tranont "has helped me grow as a person. It has helped me grow as a leader. It has helped me to be a servant to others." The notion of serving through example hits the objective of Tranont squarely on the head. A wide range of personalities are brought together under one umbrella, to enhance the experience of all. Farfan credits her time with Tranont as having stimulated "incredible personal growth."

In a few words, though a few words could never do her justice, Cindy Farfan is a prime example of what the incredible, indefatigable spirit animating Tranont can do for everyone who holds within herself the courage to follow her dreams.

Kurt Hawks

A salesman for the last two decades and some change, Kurt Hawks was first introduced to Tranont through Ron Glover (refer to Chapter 3 above) and has been involved with the company since the beginning in October 2013.

Hawks is most strongly drawn to Tranont's ideals of financial empowerment, financial education and the direct sales model which allows for the rapid construction of a powerful residual income engine. Selling products directly to a consumer or a business, while earning an ever increasing amount of residual income, is one of Tranont's features Hawks calls "unique." This is one of many aspects that separate it from other multi-level marketing (MLM) companies.

Hawks goes on to claim that, of those financial services companies with which he is personally and professionally familiar, the majority of Tranont's supposed competitors offer no real way to earn a substantial income without tying oneself down with red tape. In order to participate in a usually less-than-stellar compensation plan, you would have to sort through and sign up for a whole host of insurance and securities licenses. The worst part is that there are very few real opportunities to become truly profitable at the end of such a road.

Tranont's dual compensation plan, however, allows its representatives to start selling non-licensed products right off the bat. Even as an associate is learning the ropes, he or she can develop what Hawks calls "direct sales income" without needing to become a financial expert. Tranont associates choose their level of involvement with various aspects of the company, and that's a huge plus as far as Hawks is concerned.

He values Tranont's non-aggressive approach: "we have financial education and other products that people need and we're not trying to sell" products and services that "aren't necessary." In other words, this company wants to put out vital information, products and services that will be of great benefit to many different types of entrepreneurs and self-starters out there. Hawks sees Tranont as the solution to the lack of satisfaction in one's generation of income. The company's products translate directly into a greatly enhanced income.

"I enjoy what I do albeit I don't have the ability to earn unlimited residual income with my current company. So in a year, I see myself making several thousand dollars a month in Tranont. And then in three years, I believe that I will be in excess of $10,000 a month. In five years, $50,000 plus a month."

Hawks expects Tranont to grow into a "multibillion dollar company" within the next few years. For this reason, in conjunction with his own drive and ambitions, he knows that his future in his industry looks like it will turn out impressively, to say the least. Imagine earning $50,000 or more per month! (For the record, I don't doubt him for a minute.)

HOW TRANONT HAS RAPIDLY CHANGED THE LIFE OF KURT HAWKS

Tranont has "made me really look at how important paying attention to your financial situation is." Hawks believes that most people harbor a "false hope that, one day, things are going to work out" by some magic trick or miracle. He adds that, "the reality is, if we don't plan for our future, it's not going to be what we want it to be." Thanks to Tranont's guidance, Hawks has learned to pay much more attention to the intricacies of money management but to also, in general, keep a weather eye on the horizon. He thinks "a lot of people are pretty good at making money, but they're even better at *spending* it."

Boiled down, Tranont taught him to strike "a healthy balance," and it is this ability that Hawks sees as the most valuable tool added to his income generating arsenal.

Hawks takes great pride in the fact that "we're actually helping the people, put[ting] them in a better position..." Those who work with Tranont "don't have a garage full of soap or products or juice or something like that. But they have an investment plan where their money goes in and they actually still have their money — and it's growing." He believes Tranont will be a "household name within five years," or possibly ten. It will revolutionize the financial industry.

> "It's the real deal. Dare to dream. There are too many success stories here. If they put in the work, it's going to pay off and they can hold their head high… look, you can go out and make a great living here, whether you recruit anyone or not… You can make six figures here… That, to me, is the success of a real, good business."

Scott Webb

No stranger to earning a multiple six figure income, Scott Webb has been in the insurance and securities industry for 23 years. Over the course of his career, he has had quite a lot of experience in agency building, helping recruit and train over 6,000 people. The success of each individual depended, he admits, on his or her personal drive to excel. Another common factor leading to failure was the lack of names available. Agents would often run out of names to call for the purposes of recruitment and/or making a sale. Without referrals, eventually every well will run dry, and nobody really likes to make cold-calls.

With these traditional flaws of multi-level marketing entities in mind, one of the key aspects that drew Webb into work with Tranont was the business model. Conferring directly with the cofounders of the company, he was introduced to Tranont at the point of its kickoff in January of 2014. Once he explained the finer points of the Fast Start Program he had been using throughout the entirety of his career, he stated that he would like to join this program with Tranont in hopes of furthering its mission. To Webb, it was vital that anyone who joined Tranont could sit down with a financial professional within one week of signing up and get started on their own personally designed financial plan to give them direction, focus and understanding of where they need to be at retirement. Thus, a strong partnership between Tranont and Webb was formed.

Because of his wealth of experience in the field, Webb, in concert with one of his close friends, Bill Ray, next wrote the compensation plan for Tranont Life. Webb proudly claims, "we were able to write a compensation plan better than anything that I've ever seen or been a part of in my career."

In addition to these points, Webb is intensely interested in the prospects of Tranont's salability. He was informed that several potential buyers are chomping at the bit to snatch Tranont Life, LLC up once it is put up for sale. The reason for the sale is simple: the resultant, huge influx of capital will fill the pockets of the company and its agents. Thirty percent of the proceeds would go directly to the people who make Tranont great (of which group anyone could be a part!). Once the company hits a retail value of one billion dollars, its sale will enrich all of those who participated in its rise to the top. "I've always wanted a chance for a piece of ownership."

Though he was earning "several hundred thousand a year pretty much whether I did anything or not," Webb sold his previous company to join Tranont and "start over." For him, *building a business* is a thrill, incomparable to anything else, really.

In the financial services industry, Webb specialized in team-building. He brings that same skill set and his own, unique energy to the recruitment process.

He claims that, in his understanding, "the average MLM person lasts about 90 days [on the job] and doesn't make much money." To Webb, it was so important to find a way to speak directly to such an individual, to "get in that person's head." That's where the financial professional aspect comes into play. If, within the first week or two of being welcomed into the fold at Tranont, the recruit was given helpful advice and educational tools to set up a retirement plan to suit his or her needs, then he or she would have already gained enough value from Tranont to justify the time spent. Furthermore, if the recruit "ever left the company, they at least get a plan that they never would have gotten before, and it's going to help get them through retirement..."

Webb takes great pride in the fact that "we're actually helping the people, putting them in a better position financially..." Those who work with Tranont "don't have a garage full of soap or products or juice or something like that. But they have a long term savings plan where their money goes in and they actually still have their money — and it's growing." He believes Tranont will be a "household name within five years." It will revolutionize the financial industry.

> "It's the real deal. Dare to dream. There are too many success stories here. If they put in the work, it's going to pay off and they can hold their head high... look, you can go out and make a great living here, whether you recruit anyone or not... You can make six figures plus, here... That, to me, is the success of a real, good business."

Personally, Webb sees himself sticking with Tranont for many years to come. In fact, he affirms, "I'm not going anywhere. I'm not retiring. I got some big goals." And Tranont, he knows, can help him realize those dreams of his.

HOW TRANONT HAS RAPIDLY CHANGED THE LIFE OF SCOTT WEBB

Tranont "has given me renewed energy... I was kind of in a 'sit-back-and-just-collect-mode in my life and now I'm energized again... I'm excited. I've got my family in the business." Webb's 24-year-old daughter, Kelsi, and 21-year-old daughter, Tasha, have joined him in his adventure, both are Jeep qualifiers and are achieving success. His two sons, Austin (serving a mission for the LDS church) and Cameron (Junior in high school), also can't wait to work alongside dad: "They love what Tranont does for families." Webb's wife, Tiffani, said, "I love the new energy Tranont has brought into our family. I love working along side our children, dream building and setting goals with our kids. We believe anything is possible here if we help enough families change their lives for the better."

In summation, Tranont has "changed my life." Scott Webb has a whole new lease on life, and Tranont could not be happier, its mission fulfilled through yet another success story.

KRISTI YOUNGBLOOD

A former network marketing professional, Kristi Youngblood worked for Sears Credit Central and insurance brokerage Sedgwick James, for four years each. She also has experience in the title industry, through Alliance Title and Escrow. From 2006 onward, she refashioned herself into a network marketing entrepreneur.

Due in no small part to her wealth of experience building businesses and assuming leadership roles, Youngblood has been approached with many opportunities over the past decade. The other quality that attracts opportunities to Youngblood (and vice versa) is her love of all things finance, taxes, savings and making money. When she was told of Tranont by her boyfriend, Jake Zabala, who is a close, personal friend of Ron Glover's nephew, she was immediately intrigued by the financial products on offer, including the 10 percent-off-the-top incentive for bringing in a merchant account.

Youngblood is nothing if not methodical. After hearing Jake Spencer speak in Boise, Idaho, she devoted a full month to researching Tranont. She was ecstatic with what she had found. On July 3, 2015, she joined "a company that I can be proud to represent." What drew her to the company was the liberty ingrained in its philosophy. For her the freedom to choose which services and products you want to represent while helping people with budgeting and taxes is simply phenomenal. Like so many other veterans of the network marketing and MLM industries, she is definitely happy with leaving behind those assignments that required her to sell "one juice or a bundle of pills that everybody has to take." She revels in the wide variety of avenues open to her through Tranont. Teaching people, giving them the tools to improve their financial positions by guiding their everyday decisions, that is the most valuable aspect of the opportunity offered by Tranont, according to Youngblood. Passion is what guides her, as evidenced by her statement, "I will not join a company if I'm not going to use the products. And I've had to decline on a couple companies because I'm like, 'I would never drink that; I would never use that; or, I don't like that makeup.'"

Though it has only been a short time since she signed on, Youngblood has already been hard at work bringing together a talented, dedicated team of five. She relates that they were all "very, very impressed" with what they saw, which is how she was able to so quickly schedule meetings and get the proverbial ball rolling.

Youngblood also deeply appreciates the flexibility inherent in structuring a business under the umbrella of Tranont. With a good-humored laugh, she says, "I've never had that before, where you can just get things done with a phone call. It's like, 'Wow, that was easy!'... There isn't, lik, a line where it's like, 'Okay, we are the owners, we are the CEOs, we are the vice presidents and you all work for us.'" Tranont treats its associates with dignity and respect, extending the hand of friendship. Thus, the second tenet of Tranont Youngblood is extremely grateful for is the culture of widespread equality, that spirit that defines what makes America great.

"In Tranont, every single person can benefit from the product. Every single person... Tranont is there for [its associates], so they can make money, save money, protect their money and have a financial future that they can look forward to... [Tranont] is going to change the way people think about finances, the way people think about their future, the way people think about the world"

No one could deny that Youngblood is ambitious. When asked what her five-year goal includes, she confidently asserts that she will reach Tranont's CEO rank within one year. Chuckling, she adds that she might be retired in five.

Youngblood believes that, within half a decade, Tranont will gain enough traction to overheaul the banking, financial and insurance industries. She says, "I think it's just like a penny doubled every day. By day 31, it's over $10 million, you know?" Tranont, essentially, is "compounding people into this idea, this belief [that] there is something more and we need to take it into our hands because what's been happening isn't working." Lamenting the fact that so many Americans retire with next to nothing by way of savings or assets, Youngblood expresses her gratitude for Tranont's suite of products as well as its educational services. Tranont gives each of us the power to reshape our destinies.

How Tranont has Rapidly Changed the Life of Kristi Youngblood

After years in the MLM industry, Youngblood had been looking for a change in style. She needed something to keep her and her family going, something she could be proud to devote herself to. When asked how Tranont changed her life, she says, "the universe answered" her call.

Since joining Tranont, she has had friends and relatives rally to her side to partake in this opportunity. Her son, for example, has been inviting his friends into the fold. Youngblood's zeal is inimitable: "It's like all I think about is Tranont, Tranont, Tranont. Who can I talk to? How many lives can I change?"

Youngblood's first concern is caring for her family. "I wanted to teach my kids first of all that they can do more than just go to school, go to college, get a job, go to work until about 70 and retire," she says. She credits the sweeping shift in the fortunes of her family to simply "being patient and waiting for the right company to come along." Now, with Tranont, a "new, incredible journey" is about to start. Youngblood adds, "now I finally have something that I'll be able to pass on to my kids and that I can help my parents with or my friends with. So, it has been one of the most positive impacts on my life."

JOHN ACQUISTO

With over 30 years of experience in the insurance and mortgage industry, John Acquisto successfully achieved nearly everything he set out to achieve, at least so he thought before crossing paths with Tranont. Through one of his neighbors, Acquisto became acquainted with Tranont's extraordinary opportunity. He states one of the main reasons that drove him to Tranont was "I liked the concept of working with people and working with money. I've worked with money my entire life and it's something that I understand." Being able to help people gain the same understanding that he had, an understanding that has helped him have a financially successful life was a thrilling idea to him.

To Acquisto, the one thing he didn't like about MLM's was that, in most cases, they have amateurs selling the products. He states "Amateur salesman do a poor job. They're usually too desperate to sell so they oversell, they overpromise, and ultimately, under deliver." What makes Tranont different from the rest is that "We refer clients to our partners. They then have a professional salesperson who works fulltime for that company sell the product; a sales person who has been trained in selling that particular product or service and knows how and when to close. That's the difference." Acquisto loves the fact that "I don't have to know everything about the product. I just have to know what my client is interested in and I make the referral and get a nice check every month."

For those considering Tranont and its unique opportunity, Acquisto wants them to understand the concept of re-directional selling. "We are taking products and services that people are already using and offering them either a better product or similar product at a considerably lower price and without a contract." Tranont allows Americans to make an income off of helping their family and friends save money on services and products they already use.

Within the next five years, Acquisto sees Tranont being the financial answer to everybody in the United States. "They offer financial education, financial tools, residual income, and most importantly, they show us how to manage and invest the money afterwards so we don't lose it." He knows this because he is now experiencing this first hand in his own life. Personally, Acquisto sees himself almost to the point where he can retire comfortably again. He recalls having lost over half a million dollars when 2008 hit. He states: "I'm at the age that I want to retire." And with Tranont, he finally sees how he is going to be able to do so. "I've been trying to replace what I lost during the recession of 2008 and I'll tell you what, the business is growing. Every single week the checks are getting bigger and bigger and I'm just loving it!"

How Tranont has Rapidly Changed the Life of John Acquisto

"You know, Tranont has made everything a whole lot easier. We've got a nice income coming in on a monthly basis which continues to grow every month. I have time to spend with my wife. In fact, right now I'm taking her to a doctor's appointment and if I was in an office someplace, I wouldn't be able to do that. So I have the freedom to do the things I want to do. I have the ability to earn the income I've always wanted to earn and get the satisfaction of helping my friends do the same."

"Five years from now, I think I'll have the financial freedom to walk away if I want to. My wife tells me I'm going to die at work because it's all I do, but I mean, I love to work, but I also love to play, and with Tranont, and the residual income it provides, it will allow me to see the world with my wife and give me the time back to do so." Tranont truly allows Americans to use the time they would have spent at the office or on sales call, and instead, give that time to the things that matter most. Acquisto concludes by saying "You know, Tranont has made everything a whole lot easier. We've got a nice income coming in on a monthly basis which continues to grow every month. I have time to spend with my wife. In fact, right now I'm taking her to a doctor's appointment and if I was in an office someplace, I wouldn't be able to do that. So I have the freedom to do the things I want to do. I have the ability to earn the income I've always wanted to earn and get the satisfaction of helping my friends do the same." As you can see, Tranont truly allows one to *Change Life*.

JULIET PECK

A single mother with six children, the story of Juliet Peck is one of triumph as well as hardship. In fear of losing her home, she works with her kids, some of whom are in college, some of whom are in high school, to hold on to the family residence. Tranont is giving the Pecks the chance not only to protect what is theirs but to fulfill their wildest dreams by helping them become truly financially independent.

Thankfully, her tale is ultimately one of hope. Peck has 25 years of experience in the real estate finance and management industry, which made her a highly desirable asset to Tranont. Her friend and neighbor, the oft-quoted and referenced Ron Glover, introduced her to the opportunity presented by the company in September of 2014. It was not a hard sell. Peck took to the message immediately, completely trusting Glover's advice. Her trust was validated when she accompanied him to meet the officers and owners of Tranont.

Peck admits to a certain amount of disenchantment with the industry she worked in previously: "After the real estate crash in recent years, I wanted something a little bit fresh that could utilize my talents and understanding of the financial world, but would be less volatile to the influx highs and lows of the real estate market. I felt like Tranont offered that when it offered product that everybody needed, that had a larger draw and a larger audience as a potential client."

What Peck most appreciates about what Tranont has to offer clients can be summarized in words: necessity and presentability. As she explains it, "the product is priced conservatively and is absolutely needed by every consumer… It's not an overpriced product or lotion, or a potion that you have to try and convince someone [to buy]."

"The owners of Tranont have put together a business opportunity that you can invite your friends to come and learn, come and expand themselves, come and broaden their horizons and their understanding about some of the things that are hard and are hurtful or frustrating in their own life. And [you know that] there's people available and that will be around you to help you grow and understand for your own benefit and allow you to have opportunities to find ways to improve your financial life."

Peck's life goals line up perfectly with the philosophy of Tranont. In light of her experiences over the course of her career and her more recent money troubles, more than anything, she wants to work with other single mothers to provide a support system that they can use to improve their financial conditions and release some of the stresses in their lives. That way, Peck reasons, "they can get out of the financial hole that they [find themselves in] and earn money little by little and improve their family life." With Tranont as a partner, she feels confident that she can empower herself and others like her. She fully expects the company will be a household name in five years or less, given how powerfully it has impacted the lives of everyday Americans all across the country.

HOW TRANONT HAS RAPIDLY CHANGED THE LIFE OF JULIET PECK

The benefit that working with Tranont has bestowed upon Peck's life is twofold. Firstly, she now has a "mechanism" that has allowed her to increase her understanding of the financial world through comprehensive education. Secondly, Tranont has injected hope into her life, hope that she can "work diligently towards a goal" and meet, or exceed, said goal. Affirming that she intends to keep her home *and* build real wealth once she restores balance to her situation, she states that she and her children "plan on making this our life and we plan on pulling out of the very ugly card that we drew and becoming a powerhouse, and helping many, many other people along the way. That's our biggest goal, it's to help others"

Karen Miller

Having studied applied sciences at NIC, once out of school, Karen Miller became a medical administrative assistant. Over the course of her career, she has worked for the local sheriff's posse and charitable auctions. It was her husband who first introduced her to Tranont in December 2014. Her husband had been brought in by Troy Stevens.

While in no way complaining about her old life, it's clear that Miller definitely appreciates the renewed sense of vigor animating her activities. Where before she had been a slave to the grind, now she is free to pursue goals she sets for herself. In the end, she wants nothing more than to put in place, for herself and her son, the most secure financial future possible, and the education provided to her by Tranont is allowing her do just that. Actually, because of the degree to which her own financial situation has taken a turn for the better, she now looks forward to giving others a leg up just as she was given.

Miller hits the nail on the head when she states that middle class in America is in trouble. "We work really hard for what we have," she says, "and we're probably the most taxed. And we're the least educated on financial [issues]." That's why she's so thankful that Tranont offers a host of educational tools. The accessibility of these products ascertains that everyone can learn invaluable lessons that empower them to a build lasting wealth for themselves and their families. Miller's end goal is identical to that of Tranont. In her own words, "I know my parents didn't know how to save for retirement or even how to invest or any education. So to know that I can help educate people and help change people's lives, it is now become my mission."

> "I very much believe in Mr. Berry's vision. I have watched a lot of friends and family not be able to save for retirement, not have any savings and just lack of education. And the chance to help everybody I know and love really made me passionate about [working with Tranont]. To know that I can help people is just huge for me. And [so was] the chance for me to teach my son better and to kind of stop the transition of, you know, [poor financial planning,] from generation to generation... this is the most amazing company I've ever seen or been a part of and it truly is going to change your life for the best."

The path of Tranont can lead only onward and upward. According to Miller, "Tranont is going to grow by leaps and bounds." She expects them to be the best MLM company in existence within a few years because of their commitment to giving average, everyday Americans the chance to seize a great future. Having experienced the tremendously powerful effects Tranont can have on a life, Miller finds herself in no position to doubt that millions could reap the same rewards.

How Tranont has Rapidly Changed the Life of Karen Miller

In the short seven months that Miller has been involved with Tranont, her life has completely changed. Liberated from the doldrums of her uninspiring former career, she admits that now, "I eat, drink and sleep Tranont and it keeps me up at night. Literally, you know?"

What she loves most of all is the chance to positively affect the lives and livelihoods of those around her. These days, she is always asking herself, "Who can I help next? Whose life can I help change?" This has made all the difference in the way in which she interacts with her social and professional environments and the world at large.

Troy Stephans

Ron Glover first introduced Stephans, a commercial airline pilot, to Tranont in October of 2013. What most powerfully drove him to tie himself to Tranont's train was the company's vast experience in the network marketing arena. He wanted to flex his muscles on the financial side of things and see his way to making it big while working with a top leader in the industry.

Being able to help people attain their financial goals through services like cell phone coverage, merchant processing and background checks is very important to Stephans. He is also quite happy with the fact that no elaborate sales pitches are needed; joining Tranont just makes good sense. In his own words, "A lot of [business owners] are already using the services [that Tranont offers]. We're just going to show them a better way."

According to Stephans, you can't go wrong with Tranont if you are looking either to supplement your income on a part-time basis or create the foundation for the continuous and potentially massive accrual of real wealth. In the next three to five years, Stephans sees himself continuing on a path of serving others, of helping them to achieve their own financial goals. Self-improvement through Tranont's educational courses is an integral part of that process.

Tranont has set itself far ahead of the competition. Stephans explains, "I think what makes the difference is we have some very attainable bonuses." He firmly believes that Tranont will, within a handful of years, be a widely-recognized name on both the national and international scales: "Tranont could be setting new records and breaking new records for growth in the next three to five years."

> "In the next one, [or] three to five years, I think Tranont can be a recognizable name nationally on the MLM circuit..."

HOW TRANONT HAS RAPIDLY CHANGED THE LIFE OF TROY STEPHANS

Thanks in part to the financial education he received from Tranont, and in part to the perks of the JeepTM Program, Stephans has been given the freedom to pursue "an opportunity that makes me feel that if I put some time and effort in, I can help a bunch of people." Tranont offers so much to Americans. Families can rely on the security provided by the strongest financial retirement plans, each of which is tailor-made for the individual in question. Stephans has been able to help his own family feel more secure in this ever-changing world.

ZENO COHEN

Originally from the Caribbean, Cohen wanted nothing more than to help his "struggling" friends make good money. He speaks of how tough winter can be in Coeur d'Alene, and how he wants the futures of family members and friends to be secure. A massage therapist for

22 years, he admits the last decade of his life has been filled with trials and tribulations.

Tranont showed him a new way, a better way. Fresh to the game as recently as June 4, 2015, Cohen excitedly tells the tale of his meteoric rise through the ranks. He asserts that "within 24 hours, I had almost 12 people in my organization and I was like, holy crap, this is ridiculous. I've never seen anything grow this fast." Cohen actually broke a company record, qualifying for the JeepTM bonus within four or five days of signing up to join Tranont. He was given an award and recognized for his stellar achievements, but he didn't stop there! Less than three weeks later, he had nearly 30 people under his wing. His goal is to keep putting the good word out there, "spreading it like wildfire." He says, "I almost hope I get telemarketers calling me so I can get them to sign up."

Cohen admits to spending a lot of time on his phone, but he loves talking to people. Being able to reach out to people has reinvigorated him and reshaped his career path. Simply put, he calls his experience with Tranont "awesome."

> "I started off with it just as something that I could do as a part-time income and something that hopefully will start to build. But the way I'm seeing it now, I'm going, 'You know what? I can work my fulltime job doing massage while I'm building my part-time retirement or my part-time fortune and… still help people."

Cohen has always been keenly interested in learning more about the financial industry. He laments that "financial education is lacking [in this country], especially in our elementary and high school[s]." Thus, he has taken it upon himself to aid Tranont in its mission of teaching Americans to put the "live" back in "make a living." Currently, his bills are paid and his part-time, Tranont-boosted business is growing. Best of all, he can now treat his massage therapy practice more like a fun hobby. With both incomes, he is doing very, very well, which frees him up to actually enjoy his work. Thanks to Tranont, he has remembered why he got into the massage business in the first place, nearly 20 years ago.

When Cohen was introduced, through a friend, to Ron Glover, he was skeptical at first. But he approached the meeting with an open mind and soon found that the opportunity that stretched out before him was real. He *could* expand his horizons beyond anything he ever dared dream before.

Right out of high school, Cohen ran into financial trouble. Credit card and other debts hung over his head like a skyline threatening to fall and crush him. These debts pursued him throughout his life, an ever-present dark cloud that darkened his every day. Ron Glover presented the solution in the form of signing up with Tranont. And we have already seen how well Cohen did, right out of the gate.

He credits his success to his attitude, but also to Tranont's own code. The company is not "selling a product that people don't already use," as he puts it. Instead, associates are providing consumers with *essential* products and services. People *do* already use the tools. The difference is that Tranont offers these much more sensibly and cost-effectively. Cohen puts it best when he explains, "You're just saying, 'hey, look, you're already doing this. Let me save you some money. Let me redirect your spending. Let me free up some cash so that you can invest... [and] do all these things that you've been wanting to do.'"

At his first home meeting, not too long ago, a whopping 15 people showed up. Drawing that big of a crowd to a simple, low-key function is very impressive. Even better, eight of these folks (that's over half, for those of you keeping score at home) decided to sign up with Tranont even before the end of the week. Cohen states, "That's the problem I'm finding is [sic] I don't have enough hours in the day to talk to people." He wishes there were a way to "buy more hours in a day."

Another of Cohen's advantages is his innate affability. He has no problem approaching people from all walks of life. He reports, "I'm talking to business owners. I'm talking to single moms. I'm talking to everybody I can... I don't care how busy you are." That really is the Tranont way. Spread the word. Recruitment, after all, can be done at all hours.

Cohen's preferred method is to simply walk up to just about anybody and extend his hand along with a business card. One example he provides is that of a young couple he overheard talking about the lack of quality customer service pervading so many industries in this country. He told them they were just the sort of people he would love to work with, and the rest, as they say, is history.

Cohen is a "big believer" in American author, salesman and motivational speaker Zig Ziglar's principle of going out into the world and helping as many folks as possible achieve their personal goals. Doing so is its own reward, of course, but it can also lead to one's own success. It has definitely helped Cohen reach new heights. He happily proclaims, "I don't think I will ever have to worry about anything, and neither will my grandkids."

In so far as retirement is concerned, Cohen's dream is to build a home on a "little piece of property" back home, in the Caribbean. He sees himself at the helm of "a little boat," sailing at his leisure. Retiring into a life of quiet luxury, however, assumes that he can give up the drug that is the boundless energy with which Tranont has supplied him.

Preferring to end his statements on a hopeful note, Cohen tells us that, "No matter who's in charge of the government, I think [everyone] need[s] some financial help." Tranont, he assures us, is the solution to this nationwide problem. He adds that, within the next few years, "I see Tranont being a multibillion dollar company." With that added reach, Tranont could help just about anyone achieve the level of freedom he or she desires and deserves. The company has already been working wonders in just a couple of short years.

HOW TRANONT HAS RAPIDLY CHANGED THE LIFE OF ZENO COHEN

The last decade, Cohen admits, has proved the toughest of his life. But, thanks to Tranont, "I feel hope again and I'm — I'm almost in tears just thinking about it... I was at a point where I just felt like I was on a hamster wheel running and not going anywhere and I feel like I have been given an injection of hope."

MARLIN JENSEN

With a background in construction real estate sales focused along the Wasatch Front in Salt Lake County, Utah, Marlin Jensen developed, built and ran an RV park. After returning to the United States, he was introduced to Tranont by Ron Glover. He signed up in November of 2013.

Jensen lost money in the Stock Market in both the 2001 and 2008 crashes. Having been burned more than a few times through no fault of his own, he can't really be blamed for his reticence to enter into wide-eyed ventures without some persuasive arguments being made. Though new to the MLM game, he had some very good friends enter into business selling supplements and products of a similar nature. He wished them well, but refrained from joining them. That decision proved wise; the implosion of the business came shortly after he was invited into the fold.

Tranont, however, offered Jensen a whole new perspective. He saw immediately how this company was completely different than all those that he had come across before. In his own words: "I like the fact that we're not selling a vitamin or a juice or something… whose price has been ratcheted up in order to make commissions beneficial to those who are involved" in hawking the products. Those opportunities Jensen calls "typical MLM" differ wildly from Tranont, which "is actually looking at it from a different standpoint, trying to find ways to actually save people money on things they're currently spending money on now."

Jensen praises the "integrity of the company and the people behind it." The facet of Tranont he most respects is its "passion for helping people change their own lives through education and smarter financial decisions." Engineering new ways to help families save money and build relationships is what it's all about.

His personal ambitions include being able to act as he sees fit, to direct a company in exactly the way he wants to, rather than having to obey the whims of another. And he is well on his way to accomplishing just that:

"I don't necessarily have to make a million dollars a year or anything of that nature but I see myself in five years as being able to do the things that are important to me versus getting up to pay the bills so to speak or feed the beast… I think more and more people are starting to tune in that insurance contracts afford a safe and smart way for people to leverage [their assets and build wealth] throughout their lifetime[s]."

Jensen, like so many of his associates, deems not only possible but probable Tranont's goal of achieving a valuation of a billion dollars or more in the next five years. The company is, by all appearances and expert assessments, very far from reaching a ceiling of any kind.

HOW TRANONT HAS RAPIDLY CHANGED THE LIFE OF MARLIN JENSEN

He admits to being a little bit more "conservative" these days, making use of Tranont's financial products to inform both his investment and business decisions. Decisions he previously "wouldn't think twice about" he now takes the time to consider with greater care. This higher degree of focus and reflection has "made me a better student of not only what's going on in my local area, but within the state [and] within the U.S. borders." He has even taken a new approach to thinking about "world events," citing the way global markets are reacting to the financial turmoil bubbling in Greece. Informing himself to a much greater extent than he might have done previously, Jensen is now armed to better weather any storm, no matter its scale.

CONRAD CONAN

Having been with Tranont only a month, Conrad Conan nevertheless has great expectations for the company. A business development director by trade, what drove Conan to Tranont in the first place was its concept, how it offered "a variety of service" which enabled each partnered business "to choose, a la carte, one service or combination of several services." This model fosters diversification and growth, both very attractive to a man of Conan's stature.

When asked about Tranont, he extols the company, noting that "an opportunity like this is very rare and to be able to have a company that has a good business plan, a solid business plan, and has the foresight to be able to grow as the market and industry is changing," is absolutely vital to the potential for long-term success of the American business owner.

Conan unequivocally states that, five years from now, he sees himself working fulltime with Tranont. Self-described as "new to the business," he knows there are so many opportunities for growth open to him. He feels confident that, once he has more fully explored the waters of MLM, he will let go of his other ventures and completely commit himself to Tranont's vision. Partly, he is motivated by the degree to which he will able to enrich his own life. But what really excites him is the potential of Tranont to become a truly global powerhouse of a company.

Conan started with Tranont because of the respect he holds for his friend, Ron Glover, as well as the rest of the team based out of Coeur d'Alene and its environs. Conan firmly believes that, if Tranont can successfully position itself throughout the rest of the country, there is no real limit to what could be achieved. He cites the leadership of Jake Spencer as fundamental to the success of the enterprise.

"[Tranont] has given me a bigger perspective... There's hope in Tranont for people that are just starting."

HOW TRANONT HAS RAPIDLY CHANGED THE LIFE OF CONRAD CONAN

Tranont has reinvigorated Conan's approach to his career. He now looks at his daily activities as "exciting" and filled with "hope" for a better future. The rewards the company offers for simply enriching one's life and helping others to do the same are exceedingly attractive. They give people like Conan something to strive for, something more than worthwhile: a sense of fulfillment, both financial and personal.

ERIC EMERY

With a wealth of retail experience under his belt, Eric Emery defines his profession as door-to-door sales. Even when between jobs, he puts his skills to use selling products on Craigslist.

He first discovered Tranont through his grandmother and uncle. His grandmother, Deon, was the one to set up a meeting with Ron Glover, whom Emery had briefly met once or twice before. At the time of writing, Emery had been with Tranont for fewer than two weeks, but he was already amped up and "getting my gears going."

It was primarily his many years of work in the sales industry that drew him to Tranont. Because of the knowledge he had developed over the course of his spirited sales ventures, Emery was able to more fully grasp the opportunity that lay before him. He states, "I had worked in a networking marketing company before and I knew the power of it, and I've always, since the first time I was ever introduced to it, been a huge fan of residual income."

Tranont seems to have created the perfect model for generating that coveted and eventually self-replenishing resource. From the first time he logged on, Emery saw the potential for building last wealth. Just about anyone, even those lacking his strong background in sales, could forge a powerful, income earning machine on a part-time basis. Important to him is the knowledge that he and his associates are selling products that will actually help people, regardless of whether they are planning to start a business or not. The financial education services on offer ensure that anyone, business owner or not, will be able to revolutionize and streamline his or her personal finances. Of course, entrepreneurs stand to gain the most from Tranont's suite of products, but Emery really appreciates the ways in which the company can benefit just about anyone.

"I love helping people, and the fact that even the base products [of Tranont], without doing anything on the business side, is [sic] going to make people save so much money [attracted me to the company]."

Given how busy the average American is today with all those tasks and chores, Emery found Tranont's easy-to-follow and highly informative presentations to be a breath of fresh air. Where other companies might require you to study for impossibly dense material for hours and hours with no real end in sight, Tranont keeps it simple. The resources you need to succeed are already within you, and Tranont professionals guide you through the entire learning process and beyond.

While both Tranont and all of its associates benefit from the influx of new recruits, the fact that the company is not solely focused on acquiring new personnel is very much appreciated by Emery. Providing support for existing members and actually selling a product that has great value are two key features that distinguish Tranont from its competitors.

Having access to such a wide array of tools, supported by such a powerful framework and such talented, committed individuals give associates a broad, diversified reach through Tranont.

> "There are so many different companies involved [in Tranont's operation] that it's pretty much like starting up 15 different businesses at once. There are different avenues you can go with, so there really is a niche, a slot for everyone, no matter what they're interested in, whether it's electronics, financial help, investing, anything like that. There's something for everyone and everyone can do it."

Emery notes the importance of working with products and services that can really benefit the average American: "you're not teaching some a new habit. You're not getting them to try a new product every day. You're not changing their daily routine." The fact that people naturally have to think about their jobs, finances and retirement means that Tranont's products are immediately useful to them. Rather than being sold knick knacks, they gain access to materials and information that they will want to absorb and digest because these actually help them. Investing the time in learning how to effectively use Tranont's products is inextricable from investing in one's own financial future.

Though he is passionate about the industry, Emery can sympathize with those who might not find finances fascinating from the get-go. However, he assures newcomers that, once they see how useful these services can be, they will sign on and become hungry for more. After all, one's financial situation affects every other aspect of daily life.

As we commonly see in Tranont associates, Emery is endowed with a giving spirit. He states, "I love meeting new people. I love strangers. I love helping people." And it is this drive that compels him to want to stay on with the company for years to come, helping bring on new people, just as he was brought on by Ron Glover.

The bold prediction that, in five years time, Tranont's current members and associates will "look back and wonder how we started so small" is one that Emery makes with the utmost confidence. He adds, "the quality of people joining right now is proof alone that this is only going to snowball into something so much bigger than anyone could imagine."

How Tranont has Rapidly Changed the Life of Eric Emery

Emery tells us that Tranont "has changed my life by renewing my trust that there's always new innovations, always new ways to do things." The power to uplift the average American family from the roiling waters of debt is what drives Emery to keep pushing himself. In addition, he is encouraged by the knowledge that others like him have already succeed through Tranont. He fully expects to do the same, and then, having risen to the top himself, he will give others a hand. In summary, he states, "Most of these new enrollments are people that already are financially set. They already know what they're doing. They've already done the work but they're just so excited to help new people even though they don't have to. That's what has really impressed me." And that's what spurs Emery to keep changing his life rapidly.

Glen Price

A 30-year veteran of the food industry, Glen Price has supplemented his income for the past 12 years through working part-time in financial services. As he himself put it, he dealt with "everything from mutual funds, annuities, life insurance, pretty much helping people with their financial education and putting together plans for them." Therefore, he is an ideal Tranont candidate, plain and simple.

Price found out about Tranont through his cousin, who claimed Tranont was "doing things totally different." Price's cousin urged him to carefully consider the offer on the table. Price took these words to heart and joined Tranont in April of 2014.

What attracted Price to Tranont initially was the smart banking concept (refer to Chapter 6), in tandem with the emphasis on building up one's personal finances in a flexible manner that is compatible with a packed daily schedule. The promise of potentially being able to own a company while not having to slave away for hours a day proved tremendously appealing. The other aspect that intrigued him was Tranont's focus on providing invaluable education to its associates. Price claims this goal of enriching the lives of average Americans allows each new associate to develop an "emotional connection" with each other and the company. Of course, the dual compensation plan is no slouch either, and he admits to finding it, too, "a very cool thing that they [the founders of Tranont] have put together there."

Price is a cautious man, advocating that anyone consider Tranont — or any other opportunity, for that matter — carefully. That being said, he assures potential new recruits that, no matter how hard he tried, he could find nothing but advantages in signing up with the company. "I would just say," he emphasizes, "really give it [Tranont] a good look before you actually turn away. You might be making a big mistake."

When asked what heights he sees himself reaching in the next five years, Price boldly asserted: "I see myself making it all the way to the top, [to] CEO." With enthusiasm and gusto like his, there is no reason to doubt him, here.

Achieving that lofty goal would be made much simpler if Tranont continues to thrive. Price gave his thoughts on the matter, stating, "I have just been amazed every single time I've gone to a regional convention… There's always something new, [a] new product, new people, new leadership." In short, he can identify no reason why he should not be able to reach (or, perhaps, even surpass) his personal and professional objectives, thanks to the utter lack of ceiling looming over Tranont.

> "I always see it moving and ongoing and I've been very pleased on [sic] how the company is steering in the right direction. I think we have incredible leadership. I think that this company can go as far as they really want to go. So I don't know. I think it could be one of the top financial companies in the nation and possibly in the world because they really focus on it."

How Tranont has Rapidly Changed the Life of Glen Price

Both Price's vision of his future and his outlook concerning money have completely changed. "I could see myself retiring sooner," he says. "It gives me more hope and opportunity that I can actually go out and do whatever I want to do and that I could be done in three years if I really wanted to. If I just want to buckle down, I could actually retire."

Bill Styles

Right off the bat, Bill Styles, a veteran financial planner who served in that industry from 1979 to 2003, calls Tranont "a perfect fit" due to his background. He has experience in both the "traditional" and "more nontraditional" spheres of the business, having spent ten years with Nortwestern Mutual, nearly ten years with MassMutual and some time with World Financial Group. On June 1, 2015, however, Styles's professional life changed dramatically for the better. That's the date he joined Tranont, shortly after being introduced to the company by yours truly.

In addition to having held a wide array of investment jobs, including in the insurance, real estate, mortgage and healthcare, industries Styles has had some prior experience with multi-level marketing. In 2003, he sold his financial practice to join a network marketing company that sold nutritional products. For a time, he made good money in this business, but found that the products offered were too niche to garner the broad appeal necessary for long-term success. The typical MLM company focuses too intently on one particular product, one that doesn't have a long shelf life. The other major problem, he reasons, is a lack of education. Though there is an opportunity to make money, Styles feels the standard way MLM is organized leaves much to be desired.

By contrast, Tranont has the financial education tools that can "meet the demands of the masses" rather than serving only knowledgeable industry insiders who need less of a leg up. Ever the pragmatist, however, Styles warns that "there is no quick success." Building a thriving business "takes work, it takes learning, it takes discipline, it takes long-term vision." His advice to Tranont's fresh, incoming talent is this: "You have to have long-term vision in order to have short-term focus. And once you can see where you're going out 3, 5, 10 years or longer, then your focus should be [on] exactly what you need to do today, this week, this month, this quarter, this year to lay a foundation [for] success." The reward for such diligence, he claims, is the privilege of partaking in an "incredible opportunity" with the potential for astronomical payoffs.

> "My long-term goals are pretty lofty in that it's not about titles, awards, and things like that. It's more about helping other people meet their financial goals and having a measure of financial self-reliance... I see Tranont emerging as a powerful force in the financial education and financial services industry."

Styles had been in the financial planning business for 24 years, which means he is definitely goal-oriented. He has his eyes on the ultimate prize. Where does he see himself in five years? With Tranont, of course. When the company becomes a household name, sometime in the next few years, Styles wants to be on board of that ship as it cruises to new horizons. And he desires nothing more than to become "one of the top leaders in the company." Proclaiming this, he quickly laughs, adding that he doesn't covet the position for the "accolades and kudos." He says he has simply been fortunate to have had a lot of great mentors provide him with training and inspiration. Mentors like Dr. Stephen R. Covey, a professor at Brigham Young University, gave Styles a "head start." One of the reasons he is so thrilled to be doing business with Tranont is that this company actually gives others the same sort of "head start" Styles enjoyed as a young man. With network marketing guidance, industry-leading financial products and, of course, top-notch financial education, Tranont provides a unique opportunity.

Styles maintains that the training offered is valuable beyond the monetary gain. In fact, it teaches "people to have bigger goals and bigger dreams" while giving them the tools to translate those dreams into reality.

HOW TRANONT HAS RAPIDLY CHANGED THE LIFE OF BILL STYLES

In summary, Tranont has given Styles the proper, optimized platform to achieve all of his personal financial goals in the next three years. That's much faster than even he, with his wealth of experience, would have anticipated. He admits, "I followed my own advice for all those years I was in the financial business and I have a good income, but I think [Tranont] will cap off my career and be able to lead other people to do the same thing," adding the admitted understatement, "I mean, I'm in pretty good shape now."

STEVE ROSS

Steve Ross has a strong background in the financial services industry, with some 14 years under his belt. Scott Webb, Ross's mentor, first introduced him to Tranont back when it was still brand new. Ross seized on the chance to become one of the company's founding members.

There are two primary reasons for his wanting to join Tranont for this grand journey, namely: ownership and a way to reach the masses. Throughout his career, Ross found very few avenues lead to real ownership, which fact is especially true for the most recent position he held, "Any entrepreneur that works hard wants to reap the reward of their efforts, if you don't get to own it, you are just an employee building up someone else's business." The ability to reach the masses, was a strong second motivation. Ross noted that, though his clients and associates typically liked the business models, and the idea of working part-time to make additional money by helping other people, his previous position only presented one way to accomplish this. You had to become a financial professional and not everyone saw themselves that way. The idea of getting licensed and learning to be an expert in that field before you could make money was intimidating. He comments, "I could never recruit those people because there wasn't really a means or vehicle, that they could do it part time without becoming an expert." Tranont has created a dual compensation wherein you can earn while you learn. In fact an associate with Tranont truly has a choice if they ever want to be a financial expert or if they just want to partner with one of the wealth specialists to accomplish the same goals, "There is a place for everyone in Tranont, people can pick and choose what part of the business they like best and focus their energies on that, and still be successful." This opportunity was not available to Ross in his previous position. Thus, he would often come across people who appreciated the services provided, but just couldn't make the leap required to see themselves as financial professionals.

In Ross's eyes, the driving force behind some folks' negative perception of multi-level marketing is the enforced necessity of artificially constructing a prohibitively large structure. That sort of burden is all too typical of the multi-level industry. According to Ross, the compensation plans of most MLM companies are "structured to where unless you have thousands of people in your organization, you're not really making much money, and often spend more that you make." This promotion of a gross unreality prevents everyday folks from gaining any traction and, thus, building real, lasting wealth.

Tranont does away with all that nonsense. Thanks to its specialized education and delivery vehicles, Tranont lets you build a company that drives your career forward and gives you a strong, viable and full-time income. From the ground-floor on up, every Tranont associate earns good, great or even astonishingly high pay. Ross happily notes that, because of Tranont's unique compensation plans, he is basically getting paid twice for the same amount of work.

> Working with Tranont, "you'll see something that reaches the masses on [a] level that no other MLM or even financial services company has ever done."

One of the indicators that Tranont occupies a more-than-enviable position in the market is the number of imitators that have arisen since its inception. Ross states that "people are already trying to duplicate what we put together," selling products as well as financial services. However, Tranont is the only company to have created a fool-proof formula that will make it an international player. Those pretenders to the throne can only spin their wheels deeper into the mud.

With the next few years looking so bright, Ross has big plans for the very near future: "I see myself at the top paid position, the CEO position... having built up a large organization and to be able to receive one of the largest payouts" expected to be distributed once Tranont hits the world stage.

HOW TRANONT HAS RAPIDLY CHANGED THE LIFE OF STEVE ROSS

Ross is used to being a big fish. The trouble is, no matter how big a fish you are, if the pond itself is huge, making waves is impossible. Ultimately, he left his previous position because, even though he brought home a very respectable paycheck, "unless you were making $500,000 or more per year you were a nobody in the company."

Now, being a big fish in a smaller pond, helping Tranont grow, gives him the chance to "shine." Since signing on with Tranont, immersing himself in its philosophy and locking ranks with this burgeoning company, he has made more money than ever before and won every incentive trip offered up to this point. Yet, it's the leadership role that sold Ross, from the beginning. He revels in the successes achieved so far, having helped to develop Tranont into an industry juggernaut, and he looks forward to those triumphs still upcoming.

BOB AND CODI THOMAS

Happily married, Bob and Codi Thomas present a different picture altogether than those we whose stories we have read throughout this chapter. For one thing, they did not, at first, see eye-to-eye about Tranont.

Bob Thomas is in the wholesale lumber business and has been consistently approached for the last 20 years by different network marketing companies. Though he personally appreciates financial products for the value they can add to an individual's portfolio, a business' vitality and the family budget, he had personally never been interested. Until Tranont came along, that is.

Introduced to Tranont by a Ron Glover, where Bob had previously been reticent to discuss this type of business venture, he admits of his old underling, "He had the ability to catch my ear." Some time later, Bob met up with Tranont's owners, whom he calls "people of integrity," and that was just about that.

Codi Thomas is a nurse by trade. She and her prior husband were divorced when her kids were still young, which spurred her to go back to school. With her nursing degree, she was able to provide a comfortable life for her family. For Codi and Tranont it was not love at first sight. She claims, "I don't have a warm fuzzy feeling about multi-level marketing." Despite the fact that her husband was earning residual income to the tune of $1,000 per month from a previous MLM venture he was involved with (this, in addition to his enterprise through Tranont, whose praises he couldn't stop singing), the ever pragmatic nurse Codi was not easily swayed.

Finally, Bob convinced his wife to go to a Friday night meeting where the concept of the Circle of Wealth was discussed. "That just completely changed my view on finances," she says. "I thought to myself, this is information I wish I would have known 30 years ago." When she first got that clear picture of what Tranont truly represents, what it stands for, she "thought this is a business I could have done as a single mom... there's something in it for everyone."

The Thomases are highly sociable people, and Tranont complements their outgoing personalities perfectly. Hosting the aforementioned Friday night meetings presents a recurring, wonderful opportunity to open their home to people. They do, in fact, have more time for non-work-related gathers, as well. Now that they no longer have to concern themselves with how they are going to retire as well as maintain their lifestyle, everything seems to be falling into place for this upbeat couple.

As of the time of writing, Bob got started with Tranont a year ago. However, it wasn't until his wife joined him as a business partner, nine months later, that he became truly active. But neither one of them has looked back since. For Bob, aside from the financial gains Tranont delivers, it's all about building relationships and exiting one's comfort zone. "No question," he says, "we're interested in making a lot of money. But we love the products, and we think the products alone can make a difference in the lives of the people we talk to about [Tranont]." There are a lot of people he and his wife want to introduce to this unique opportunity.

"We had a meeting, I would say, about a month ago. I had a guy that worked with me in my business 25 years ago… He's had some health problems, [and] they've struggled a little bit financially… He came to one of the meetings and, afterwards, he was almost emotional because he said this [opportunity with Tranont] gave him hope where he hadn't had hope in a long time. He could see himself doing this business and making money and enjoying his life again. That's the thing that is kind of like a light bulb moment for us, is if we can get involved and change peoples' lives for the better, that's the exciting thing."

All former opinions discarded, since joining Tranont, Codi has dived head-first into the pool of B2B credit card processing. She recalls one fine morning when she and her husband went to breakfast and struck up a conversation. "By the way," she casually slipped in, "who does your credit card processing?" A few short questions and answers later and another person was sold on Tranont. Now, anywhere Codi goes, the places she shops, the restaurants where she dines — every new place presents a new chance to spread the word. Her husband proudly states that "Codi is the perfect person for this business because, wherever she goes, she's got the credibility." Her newest aim is to bring in a two million dollar per month credit card processing client, and she has the skills to manage that feat. Already, Codi has, within the past weeks, closed a couple of doctors' offices, saving everyone a few thousand dollars per month.

As for the products on offer, the Thomases have nothing but praise. The OneView and tax app products are, in a word, "phenomenal" and really "make a difference in people's lives." The couple has even talked about it with their kids, including their autistic daughter, who uses OneView to collate all of her debit card and other expenses into one easy-to-use menu. Codi states: "I have a daughter, Kayci who is autistic. She is very high functioning, however, but still has never been able to budget money due to the basic conceptual deficits of an autistic person. I signed her up and introduced her to the products. She was able to grasp the one view concepts and is now able to budget her money and use a debit card. She is very capable with the computer and is able to check her account balance and the transactions there. Her only criticism being 'I have to wait until the next day to know what my balance is, Mom!' I ran that past the founders and they are working on having One View update immediately! Tranont has really helped every member of their happy family.

In the next three years, Bob says, "I see us enjoying life beyond our wildest dreams. I understand a little bit about timing and when you find the right company, in the right place, with the right people, that sort of thing… once that ball gets rolling, there's no way you could stop it, even if you tried."

How Tranont has Rapidly Changed the Lives of Bob and Codi Thomas

The Thomases have always been tight-knit, to say the least. They built their home together, themselves. Because they are so close to each other, they promptly jumped into business together. Bob claims that, now, "We feel like little kids again." Tranont, for him, is a lot of work, but nothing has gotten him more excited.

The reason for this excitement is that aspect that has profoundly changed Bob and Codi Thomas's lives. "We have a desire, a need to lift people up," Bob states. And, with Tranont, they now have the ability to help folks find money that might have been lost or transferred away. Through Tranont, Bob acknowledges, "we really can make a difference in people's lives."

Miguel Mendez

For the past 7 years, Miguel Mendez has developed his administrative acumen working side by side with directors, attorneys, and CEOs primarily in Salt Lake City, Utah, but spent time in Tucson, Arizona, and Atlanta, Georgia as well. His current role is working as an Executive Administrator & Project Manager and has worked in similar roles since 2008. Mendez was introduced to Tranont through David Adlard. At first, Mendez was reluctant to accept his invitation. At that time, he had plenty of friends and knew of co-workers that had been involved in MLM's that sold the "pills, potions, and lotions" for companies like WakeUpNow, doTerra, and NuSkin, but he had never been interested himself. Mendez states that he "never saw the point behind trying to recommend or sell something to my family and friends that I wouldn't personally use or didn't have a passion for myself." He then goes on to admit: "I was a little skeptical and hesitant to learn more, but I saw the passion and sincerity in his eyes, so I felt I should just go and check it out."

The opportunity Mendez had been searching for was beginning to manifest itself into reality. When asked about his first encounter with Tranont, he recalls being immediately convinced by not only what he saw and heard, but what he felt. Mendez went on to explain that

"Yes, I finally found an MLM that offered something I would actually use — and not just a product, but several products, and a company backed by honest and successful leaders that would teach me how to make, save, invest, and protect my money — but these weren't the reasons why I was sold." When asked to elaborate, he followed up by stating "Yes, all this was important to me and played a major role in my decision, but the primary reason that drove me to join Tranont was because of the vehicle I saw it could provide me to fulfill my real dream of becoming a motivational speaker." Mendez long held this dream from a young age, and watching the presenter speak in front of the room that night gave rejuvenation to a desire which gradually became dormant through the nine to five paradigm which entrenches so many of our fellow Americans today.

When asked what separated Tranont from the other MLM opportunities extended to him before, Mendez states that Tranont differs the most because of the unique business model it provides. Unlike most of the MLM's out there, Tranont has 3 main revenue streams: Direct Selling (Business to Business and Business to Consumer), Team Building, and Financial Professional Services. Tranont gives you the opportunity to earn while you learn. This flexibility played a major role in his decision to join Tranont. Moreover, Mendez loved the fact that Tranont wasn't selling some new energy drink, supernatural potion, magical fat slimming wraps, or fast acting diet pill. They weren't going to load up his garage with piles of boxes of superficial products nobody truly needed. Tranont's products and services fill an absolute need for every person in this country who has any hope of eliminating their debt and living the real American Dream. Mendez also loved that "What Tranont offers isn't limited to any gender, race, or demographic. Tranont is an opportunity for every American, both rich and poor, old and young, male and female, creditor and debtor; whether educated or uninformed, trained or inexperienced, Tranont invites all to partake of the wealth of information it provides and grants them the opportunity to secure a wealth of their own."

Mendez invites those who are looking at Tranont for the first time to "take away and comprehend that Tranont not only provides you with access to the products, resources, and information you'll need to create real sustainable wealth, but more importantly, it provides you with the access to some of the brightest minds in the financial industry; leaders that have already created their own wealth empire and have been wise and responsible enough to preserve and protect it." Mendez admitted that he didn't realize the enormous potential MLM's could provide to his career and opportunity for advancement. He elaborated by saying:

"That's something that people, myself included, don't initially realize when they learn about MLMs or Network Marketing opportunities. Break down each word! NETWORK. MARKETING.

Network – is the process of interacting with other people to exchange information and develop the necessary contacts with leaders that can provide you with the guidance, wisdom, resources, and opportunities you currently lack, and especially, to further one's career and expand your business.

And

Marketing – the action or business of promoting and selling products or services; but not just marketing Tranont and its amazing products and services, but marketing yourself! This is the opportunity for you to build your reputation and solidify your own credibility as a businessman, entrepreneur, and innovator; in essence, this is your chance to become "Successful", a label which so many people have sought after but have chosen to let the opportunity slip away due to the fear of failure, the ridicule it would bring, and a lack of preparedness and ambition they should have developed before the opportunity presented itself."

Within the next 5 years, Mendez hopes to travel around the country building teams, finding leaders, and inspiring them to help others do the same. Mendez has decided to translate American Dream Again and has already embarked on the Spanish translation of the book with which he plans to distribute throughout the Salt Lake Latin community and abroad as Tranont continues to grow. Mendez see's Tranont, and the Executives who brought this company to life accomplishing their goals of making Tranont a billion dollar company and sees them expanding and eventually establishing a household name and national presence in the financial arena with a continued reputation of integrity and respect as they help Americans wake up from their American Nightmare and turn their American Dream into reality.

"Tranont has the vehicle for you to reach your destination! Tranont's purpose is to provide you with the income you've always needed to do that which you've always wanted. With Tranont, no dream is impossible. Your opportunity has arrived. Act now! Tranont is not here to just help you make ends meet, but is here to be the means to an end so you can meet your dreams and manifest them into reality."

Tranont is a message of hope for the millions who find themselves overwhelmed by their current financial situation. With so little growing up, Miguel Mendez found himself with few resources as he looked to progress towards success at a young age. When his mother decided to move to Salt Lake City from New York by herself with her 3 kids, she had a mere $300 to her name. Mendez grew up watching her struggle to provide enough money to cover the basic necessities working multiple jobs for them their entire upbringing. Through food stamps, government housing, and a rare appearance of child support checks from the dad he never met, his mother managed to overcome it all without the help of a husband or a father figure in their lives to support them. She was married twice and both ended in divorce. Through the school of hard knocks, she did her best to manage her finances to make ends meet living paycheck to paycheck. Mendez says that: "Through it all, she somehow made sure she always had enough food on the table and clothes on our backs for a new school year with what little financial education she did have. I learned my hustle from her. She was both my mother and my father. I wouldn't be where I am today were it not for the sacrifices she made for me. I promised myself I would be the father that I never had and be there to provide for my own family someday." As long as Mendez could remember, he had always wanted to be a role model to those who were raised in a similar or worse circumstances than he was and show them how to overcome it. From a young age, he pictured himself speaking in front of large audiences as living proof that we can all change our lives if we set our minds to it. Through Tranont, he finally began to see how.

Mendez proclaims: "We are not merely victims of our environment or the circumstances and resources we were born with, but are living products of our thoughts, choices, and actions! We can change! We can adapt! There is a quote by Earl Nightingale that I love and live by: "We are all self-made, but only the successful will admit it". Stop justifying your failures and blaming others for your lack of achievement! We become what we think about!

Miguel Mendez concludes with these words of advice: "To anyone reading this book right now... I know what you're thinking. I know that you dream of achieving success and becoming financially free to one day be able to check off those desires on your bucket list and fulfill those ambitions you've held as a kid. The fact that you're reading this book right at this very moment tells me this is the case. Things happen for a reason. Please understand, before you go on to turn another page in this book, Tranont has the vehicle for you to reach your destination! Tranont's purpose is to provide you with the income you've always needed to do that which you've always wanted. With Tranont, no dream is impossible. Your opportunity has arrived. Act now! Tranont is not here to just help you make ends meet, but is here to be the means to an end so you can meet your dreams and manifest them into reality."

Wrapping Up the Chapter

Having put those success stories to paper leaves me wanting to just say, "wow." These folks speak more convincingly than I ever could about the powerful potential for change that Tranont represents.

You too could grab your piece of the New American Dream. Maybe you feel encouraged by the knowledge that you are not alone. I sincerely hope that this chapter has shown you how Tranont can help you achieve even your wildest financial objectives. After all, as evidenced by the tales above, the company has already done a great deal of fine work in that department.

Keep reading, because more excellent resources are on their way. In the next chapter, we will discuss the Private Banking Concept, which will provide you with the resources to really start building real wealth. True financial independence is only a few dozen pages away.

What do you say, shall we continue onward?

6.

BE YOUR OWN BANK

In this chapter, you will be presented with a rather revolutionary concept, so you may want to take a moment to brace yourself.

There is a secret history surrounding money, credit, interest and other financial concepts. Many Americans will never know the inner workings of the systems overseeing their monetary wellbeing, but you need not remain in the dark. You have made it this far, after all!

The truth of the matter is that banks, credit unions, credit card companies and other such institutions do not want you to know how to liberate yourself, because they make too much money off of your ignorance. Well, I am about to show you what they don't want you to see. In essence, you are about to enter a financial world without borders or boundaries, without controls stifling you. You are about to take your first step into a world where anything is possible. All you have to do is dream it.

In the following segments, we will review how you can build real wealth, regardless of whether we find ourselves in a Bull or Bear Market. No matter the current state of the economy, you will not only survive but *thrive*.

How, you ask? You are going to become an expert in Smart Banking Strategy. You are going to become your own banker, and your finances will become your personal bank account.

Here we go.

WHO IS IN CONTROL OF YOUR MONEY?

First, ask yourself this simple question: *do I control my own money?*

If you answered "no," you belong to the segment of the American population that encompasses the vast majority. Unless you were a naturally gifted financial savant, or you were given the best education and had insider access, you could not possibly hope to compete alone. The sad reality is that American education falls woefully and ridiculously short of even approximating teaching anyone financial literacy.

Even in Henry Ford's day, this was apparent. The American industrialist and founder of the Ford Motor Company famously said, "It is well enough that people of the nation do not understand our banking and monetary system, for, if they did, I believe there would be a revolution before tomorrow morning."

So, who *does* control your money? Well, various entities do. Two immediately apparent ones are the banks and the government.

The former hold your money, charging you an assortment of fees for that convenience. Anytime you want to take out a loan to buy a car or a home, the bank will also kindly charge you varyingly exorbitant interest rates, kneecapping your financial structure and costing you an arm and a leg.

There are other institutions, of course, to whom you are beholden for the *privilege* of accessing *your own money*. But, since you are quick on the uptake and get the picture, lingering here would serve no purpose. Therefore, we will move on to how to deal with this calamity.

WHAT IS THE PRIVATE BANKING CONCEPT?

A financial expert (say, one from Tranont) would be able to go on in much greater detail, but, in broad terms, the Private or Smart Banking Concept affords you several amazing abilities. Thanks to permanent, dividend-paying life insurance, it allows you to create your own banking system. You will have a whole new and powerful cash flow whose resources you can channel into whatever task, project or purchase you see fit.

By establishing a solid plan, you can use this method to finance car purchases or your home. If you run a business, you could even finance equipment purchases. Eventually, you will expand your system of "banks" into a grand network capable of absorbing vast quantities and different types of wealth. Never go money-hungry again!

"How do I get in on the ground floor of this sweeping plan," you ask? Well, it is beyond the scope of this book to cover this topic in the depth it is due. Thus, there will be a bit of light reading involved in order for you to amass more wealth than you might have thought possible.

THE BOOKS YOU NEED TO READ

1. Becoming Your Own Banker, by R. Nelson Nash

This groundbreaking book shows you the secret to building real wealth without relying on parlor tricks or, worse, the Wall Street rollercoaster (which, as we all know, is prone to breaking down).

A firm believer in the "Austrian School of economics," Nash is a critical proponent of individual, economic liberty and limited government. Our friend, Ron Glover, calls *Becoming Your Own Banker,* "a robust financial strategy designed to put you in control of your money."

At this point, the Smart Banking concept may seem a bit like hocus-pocus to you. Your skepticism is a valuable tool in many areas in life but, I assure you, there is no real trick to building real wealth and achieving true financial freedom. Furthermore, there is nothing illegal or shady about this subject. The strategies propounded in

Nash's book all obey the tax codes, and any other laws of the land. The difference is that, instead of passively submitting, Nash *leverages* the rules to his own advantage, which is why he has been so phenomenally successful.

You can follow in his footsteps, become financially savvy, thanks to something as simple as a *life insurance policy*. The contractual guarantees provided by life insurance can definitely be made to work to your advantage.

How would you like to *collect interest* instead of *paying it*? Glover tells us that, using Nash's strategies in conjunction with other schools of thought, we can all follow our hearts to true success. Glover states, "This concept will captivate your imagination and help you dream again. It will help you visualize a happy future. It will transport you to a whole new level, financially."

2. *The Retirement Miracle,* by National Best Selling Author, Patrick Kelly

This must-read book needs little introduction. Simply put, it will teach you how to grow your money with zero market risk. Glover "highly recommends you get this book… it is absolutely one of the best books written on this subject."

3. *Money. Wealth. Life Insurance.: How the Wealthy Use Life Insurance as a Tax-Free Personal Bank to Supercharge Their Savings*, by Jake Thompson

A number one best seller, *Money. Wealth. Life Insurance.* will demonstrate the powerful capabilities and potential cash value of the financial tool that is life insurance. The strategies outlined in this work have been used by wealthy Americans, big banks and large corporations for centuries.

The average American, sadly, was not given access to the same information. Despite its incredible, raw power, life insurance is one of the least understood tools currently available and is thus totally underused by the most folks in this country. Thompson calls for a leveling of the playing field, and I heartily concur. Leveraging life insurance should not be reserved for the elitists out there. You should have equal opportunity to make use of this amazing tool!

4. The Great Wall Street Retirement Scam: What THEY Don't Want You to Know about IRAs, 401ks, and Other Plans, by Rick Bueter

This next book jumps right in to add to the solution sought after in Thompson's work. Before, only the elite could exploit the system to achieve their full financial potential, but now you can too, thanks to this great book. Glover refers to this as an invaluable resource for discovering how to get ahold of "guaranteed income for life," which is every bit as attractive as it sounds.

The ultimate goal remains creating your own financially secure future. In a nutshell, this book explains, in terms that everyone can understand, how to build exactly such a system.

Now that we have been recommended works that present solutions, what is stopping us from pursuing these avenues to the fullest extent of our abilities? Perhaps a closer look is warranted. After all, there are some major problems facing this country.

THE BIGGEST HURDLES FACING AMERICA TODAY

The average American, usually through no fault of his or her own, lacks proper financial education. That being said, you can't be blamed for said lack if you were never given the opportunity to learn in the first place.

Here are a few facts to satiate your morbid curiosity:

- Almost everyone *finances* all of their major purchases; the average credit card debt per U.S. household is $15,270, and Americans collectively owe $856.9 billion, according to a story published by USA Today

- Interest owed to various institutions, late fees and charges, bank fees, etc., has reached astronomical heights; last year alone, Americans spent approximately $35 billion on late fees)
- The average American family unknowingly loses millions of dollars over a lifetime due to a lack of understanding of the ways in which wealth is transferred away from you, the individual, and into the grasping hands of financial institutions
- So many of us pay insane amounts of money to tax man, and what do we get out of it, really?
- Let's just reiterate that last point: *taxes are the biggest cost to the average American household*

In response to these problems, Glover states, matter-of-factly, "We need to learn how to accelerate our earnings and leverage our time." He quotes Dan Thompson, author of *The Banking Effect:* "The greatest threat to our personal financial freedom is taxes." Glover goes on to relate that the average American pays anywhere from 40 to 50 percent of their total earned income over a lifetime in taxes. That's "the largest wealth transfer" currently in play, and "It does not appear to be getting better anytime soon."

Yes, unfortunately, you did read the above paragraph right. Something like 50 percent of all of your earnings will be snatched up and put toward income, property, gas, sales and innumerable other forms of taxes.

A NOTE OF INTEREST

Aside from all of that money flying out of holes in your pockets in order to pay the multitude of taxes the government demands of you, you will also be losing massive amounts of capital on interest payments, late fees, bank fees and other charges. In fact, 25 percent of the average American's income will be lost to interest payments.

In a video entitled Smart Banking 101 (found on www.youtube.com), Glover demonstrates exactly how so much money is lost to interest. Among the examples he provides is a hypothetical (but all too frequently real) situation in which someone racks up $10,000 in credit card debt. The monthly payment might be something like $250, but only $150 of that goes towards paying the principal. The other $100 (or 40 percent of the payment) represents the cost of interest. Thus, the *volume of interest* this hypothetical individual is paying is 40 percent. Imagine how much money would be lost over the term of the loan! Assuming, of course, that this person refrains from accruing even more debt, which, given the current economy can be quite a tall order.

Another example Glover gives in that same video is a $200,000 mortgage loan, whose monthly payment amounts to $1,199. That sounds reasonable enough, right? A pretty even number that likely applies to many folks in this country. Well, in such a case, and in the earlier years of the term of the loan, the volume of interest would be $1,000. Only $199 (or 17 percent of the payment) would be applied toward the principal.

Don't confuse the *volume of interest* with the *rate,* which is irrelevant in this case. I am sure, however, that you are shaking your head in disbelief at what an outrageous cost this is. And, though this particular scenario was concocted for illustrative purposes, it is, unfortunately, quite the accurate depiction of many an American's financial state of affairs.

A rather biting quote from Albert Einstein summarizes these points best: "Compound interest is the eighth wonder of the world. He who understands it, earns it… he who doesn't… pays it."

But What About Actually Living?

You may have noticed that, even though 75 percent of your income has been accounted for already, we still haven't talked about living expenses. That's right: you will only have 25 percent, one quarter, of your total income remaining to devote to actually living. That's a pitiably small amount, isn't it? Now, perhaps you see how, despite earning a decent salary, you can really feel the pinch. The saddest part of all is that a big chunk of that last quarter of your income will need to go to buying food and other necessities, leaving little to no room for your purchasing items and services you *enjoy.*

Let me ask you this, would you not rather have this money to yourself, to spend at your discretion? Of course you would!

How Smart Banking Helps You Leap Over These Hurdles

Before you get to thinking that this chapter is going to be entirely gloom and doom, let me assure that there is an answer to all of the problems we just reviewed.

Life insurance contracts allow you to safely accumulate cash value. Your net worth won't be just a number, however, as you will retain permanent access to your capital, even while you and your family are protected by the terms of the policy. How, you ask?

Smart Banking gives you the earned interest and capital to make your purchases from *your own bank* of money rather than outside institutions. This puts you back behind the wheel of the ship you should call *My Financial Future.* Thanks to Smart Banking, your destiny can be yours to chart.

Why Smart Banking is the Answer

So many people simply have no clue where their money is going, let alone where they might safely keep it without fear of it all washing away due to maintenance fees, taxes and other concerns that tend to build up over time. General market uncertainty, a lack of safe growth options, high interest payments and abusive taxation all make for bleak prospects for the average American. But there is hope!

Smart banking gives *you* access to *your* capital, whenever and wherever you might need it. From store credit cards to car payment loans and mortgages, you will never have to worry about qualifying for credit again. Simply put, you will be paying for everything on your terms.

Think back on the figures cited above: 50 percent of every dollar earned goes to paying taxes, 25 percent to interest, and only the remaining 25 percent is money you can put toward paying your living expenses (forget about leisure and luxury!).

If you could eliminate just the 25 percent interest drain on your income, you would have 100 percent more cash on hand to devote to living expenses and items and services you might actually want to purchase. You would suddenly be *twice as rich.*

Principles of the Smart Banking Concept

Those who propagate the Smart Banking Concept steadfastly adhere to a few basic but admirable principles you should know about:

- To be the best cash accumulation vehicle for Americans
- To create uninterrupted compounding interest
- To help you avoid penalties
- To keep you from ever having to *qualify* for anything
- To ensure death benefits are passed on tax-free to your beneficiaries (your Legacy monies will remain intact for your family)
- To grant the policy owner control over how and when funds are distributed
- To, in most states, provide asset protection against creditors
- To remove the limits to how much you can invest
- To present an option that bears *no risk*

When you delve into the Smart Banking Concept, you can expect these benefits and more. You, too, can become wealthy safely *and* rapidly. On the subject of the achievability of this goal, Glover states, "You know, I see it all the time with people who created wealth, and done things right with their money throughout their lifetime. By the time they retire, they're actually making more money than they did when they were working. And that's the power of Smart Banking."

Some More Facts About Smart Banking

There are a lot of components to the Smart Banking Concept, so let's do a quick review of what we covered thus far:

- There is no risk to your capital
- You are guaranteed returns
- You will make interest payments to *yourself,* because you will take out loans from your own bank
- Your money grows for you and is used by you *tax free*
- This system immediately establishes a tax free estate
- Let's not forget that your family will be protected by the benefits of your policy
- And many more benefits will come your way

Isn't it time that you got that liquidity of capital you deserve, tax free? Consult with a specialist from Tranont. They are in the business of helping Americans just like you get set up to begin their journeys down this path.

How to Start Exploiting This Advantage

Here is what you need to know the Smart Banking process:

1. Purchase a life insurance contract from a top-rated firm
2. Fund it as soon as humanly possible
3. Gain access to capital through a collateral policy loan

4. Watch your cash values continuously grow at a variable or fixed rate
5. Repay your loans, adding the capital back in to your own account

Following these steps will build your cash reserves through investing in the safest asset in the world: the life insurance contract. This is how you *become your own* bank and control your own money, *pay interest to yourself* (and not a host of financing institutions) and *watch your money grow safely*, even as you use it.

EXAMPLES OF USES FOR SMART BANKING

What could you do with that sudden arriving and steadily growing influx of capital? Why not reduce or outright eliminate your debt? Why not finance that new car you always wanted, pay for a dream wedding (yours or your child's)? You can now afford to be lavish, if you choose. Someone (or *multiple* someones) in the family ready to head off to college? Pay for the best education money can buy, and never worry about what you will do once you retire. Anything you need to finance *now* is *now* within reach!

Protect your property investments by making your mortgage payments out to yourself. Supplement your retirement income, building a nest egg for the future (which may well be made of solid gold by the time you claim it). There is no real limit to the income potential that the Smart Banking Concept can lay at your feet.

TRANONT IS SET TO DRIVE YOU TO FINANCIAL FREEDOM

Enter Tranont. How can Tranont plug you in to this system, how can you become your own bank?

Do you remember, back in Chapter 3, when we talked about the Index Universal Life Policy, offered by Tranont Life? This product was designed to repair the financial damages incurred by Americans, who collectively lost nearly $15 trillion of their retirement funds in the most recent series of Stock Market crashes occurring over the past several years.

As a reminder, because I know we have covered a lot of information since Chapter 3:

- $100,000 invested in the S&P 500 in the year 2000 would, overall, become $126,996 by 2014.
- In the same amount of time, that $100,000 invested in Tranont Life's Index Universal Life Policy would have grown into $285,835.

There is an even more stunning difference. Are you ready? In a bad year during this period, the S&P 500 yielded a few negative returns, the worst of which was -38.49 percent. The Index Universal Life, however, bottomed out at 0.25 percent. Meaning, the worst that investment ever could have done was *earn you a quarter of a percent.* That may seem like chump change, but when compared to nearly 40 percent losses, I know where I will be casting my vote.

LET'S LOOK AT A TYPICAL AMERICAN FAMILY

Since this book is all about rebuilding America's financial future one household at a time, what better example could I give than a typical American family?

This may sound familiar to you. Here is what the financial situation of a standard 35 year old couple might look like:

- Mortgage of $227,606 at 4.25 percent, paying $1,156 per month
- First car, $11,850 at 7.99 percent, paying $526 per month
- Second car, $6,449 at 11.99 percent, paying $289 per month
- First credit card, $7,218 at 11.99 percent, paying $289 per month

- Second credit card, $2,289 at 13.99 percent, paying $92 per month

The total debt this couple has incurred up to this point is $255,412. The combined total of their payments amounts to $2,463. That's a staggering $29,556, annually.

Tranont would give this couple two options:

1. Follow the standard route, get out from under that debt at age 63 and have no significant savings or retirement fund to speak of
2. Obliterate the debt by age 44, while also generating *residual income* upon retirement.
   a. By age 50, earn $41,984 *per year*
   b. By age 55, earn $76,231 *per year*
   c. By age 60, earn $145,682 *per year*
   d. By age 65, earn $251, 534 *per year*
   e. By age 70, earn $426,736 *per year*

Who wouldn't go with option 2? Show of hands?

A Few More Morsels of Food for Thought

Before we close out this chapter, I felt we should look at a list of additional benefits the Smart Banking Concept brings to you and your family, some of which don't strictly have to do with money:

- Of course, you will accumulate cash that can be accessed tax-free
- But there are also no *minimum age or income requirements* to get started
- Gain access to your funds at any age
- You will never be forced to liquidate your account, for any reason
- In most states, you will be protected from lawsuits
- Probate is completely bypassed
- Fretting over Stock Market losses will be a relic of the past

- An annual reset provision gives you flexibility (a Tranont professional can show you how to go about it, if needed)
- Experience staggering potential for upside growth coupled with highly accurate return calculations
- Your family is protected by your policy
- Should you become disabled, your policy will remain in effect
- And, finally, though this point is probably more than obvious by now: peace of mind will be yours

Tranont Life's Index Universal Life product is proprietary. There simply is no one competing with them in this field, which just goes to show you how they stand among the few companies truly dedicated to helping you build real wealth.

In closing, an imperative from Ron Glover: "Change the way you think about money." He encourages you to move forward, to reach out to Tranont and take hold of this unique opportunity, saying, "You hold the key to your own financial future. The answer is waiting, but only for those who take action."

7 .
THE OPPORTUNITY

In the preceding chapters, we introduced Tranont and its ethical approach to business. Additionally, in Chapter 5, we told the inspiring success stories of some of Tranont's key players. Hopefully, the morals of their tales inspired you to pursue your own dreams to the fullest extent possible.

This chapter concerns itself with the opportunity that now lies before your feet. The most delicious fruit lies in the grass before you, ready for you to pick it up and take a bite. Rest assured, your eyes do not deceive you. That fruit is as real as it is nutritious, and it rolled down the hill directly over to you. How convenient! All you have to do is grab hold of it now.

I urge you to read this next chapter carefully for two reasons:

1. The information contained herein is of tremendous value.
2. Opportunities like these don't come knocking twice in a lifetime.

"While 9:00 to 5:00 and what happens in the job is important... what happens from 5:00 - 9:00 while you're off the job is INFINITELY more important."

- Zig Ziglar

Here are the steps to follow when setting out to build your New American Dream:

1. Work at your day job
2. Start and build your business in your off hours; be disciplined
3. Invest capital earned from your day job into your business
4. Once the increase in your capital intake reaches a level where you and your family can exist comfortably, you can redouble your efforts to recruit others into your camp. The best part is, helping them will help your bottom line, too!
5. Becoming really good at Step 4 will establish you as an expert in your field. When you achieve this much respected status, you will be able to teach others the means of your success. They will be more apt to believe you because of your authority. You will be fundamentally credible and, because they are more likely to join you, they are more likely to enrich themselves and you in the process.

Getting Started vs. Planning to Get Started

This statement may seem so obvious that it is needlessly inserted here, but: planning is not the same as starting. Planning is a necessary step, naturally. At a certain point, however, the baby bird has to fly from the nest. Thinking about flying forever will never beat feeling the wind beneath one's wings and learning by sense of touch.

To be sure, I am not advocating jumping out of trees or other tall places! Put those fake wings down, Icarus, because you're missing the *point*. The point is that you should plan as well as plan to start. Then, and most important of all, you should *get started*.

One Step In The Right Direction Is Worth 100 Years Of Thinking About It.

- T. Harv Eker

But How Do You Get Started?

First and foremost, the time has come to drop that stifling collar that is choking the life and vitality out of you. I am referring to that collar whose tag reads "employee." Going forward, thinking like an employee, bearing that mindset like a ship with one anchor too many, will weigh you down.

Next, you will need to find a product that inherently:

- Is recession proof, meaning that it is something people either need to have or feel they can't live without, no matter how badly they are strapped for cash
- Is sold by a company you can believe in, and one that has a track record of proven successes
- Instills passion in you and others

Do you see how choosing the right product to sell automatically ties you to a service-oriented approach? Helping others discover something to passionate about really does pay dividends.

Don't Believe the Naysayers

"Millions of people laughing in derision cannot hurt us an iota, yet we stand in absolute terror of it."

- Earl Nightingale

Though this piece of advice can be hard to swallow, depending on your particular situation, you should not listen to your detractors. Does this mean you should not listen to valuable advice or constructive criticism? Of course not. All the same, there is a world of difference between constructive criticism and someone actively treading on your dreams just because he or she is not possessed of the courage to try to break free.

Once you get started with Tranont, you will be excited to share the news, as well you should be. Be it your best friend, your wife, your younger brother or a mentor from your college days, everyone stands to respond to you differently. Here is an illustration:

Answer A: "Well, that doesn't sound so easy to me. Are you sure it's worth your time even bothering with this? I mean, it seems like a huge headache for not a lot of reward. It might not even end up working! I just don't want to see you fail."

Answer B: "That's great! That sounds like an excellent opportunity. Have you considered, though, that the market is saturated in this particular area? Maybe you could retool your focus to build a niche in such and such a way. I'm happy for you, though."

Can you spot the differences in tone? The giver of Answer B is, overall, positive while attempting to be helpful. Answer A, on the other hand, is built to convince you to quit before you start. Whom you listen to is up to you.

Michael Jordan, who needs no introduction, has something to say on the matter: "I can accept failure, everyone fails at something. But I can't accept not trying."

The above points being said, in some instances, a naysayers "naysaying" has more to do with how you approached that person. Did you exude the excited confidence you should feel in undertaking this grand adventure, or did you come across as timid and unsure of yourself? Attitude is half of everything, really.

If you have made it this far through this book, I am sure you would agree with that statement. Still, while we are on the subject of naysayers, now is a good time to talk about a common objection you are likely to hear voiced time and time again as you undertake your journey to true financial success.

About Pyramid Schemes

Many people who enter into tiered business systems similar to, but not the same as, the one offered by Tranont will be skeptical at first. Pyramid schemes are an unfortunate reality of this world, so it is wise to learn to identify and avoid these like the plague. There are many resources that can educate you further on this subject. For now, just know that the difference between a pyramid scheme and a legitimate tiered marketing initiative is akin to the difference between a toy truck and a pickup. One is a pale imitation, the other the real deal.

Pyramid schemes, which are completely illegal, by the way, sell you on commissions. Specifically, you will supposedly earn more by hiring more associates, rather than by selling more products. That seems rather backward, would you not agree? As you might imagine, it is through this particular system of "incentives" that the pyramid scheme earns its name: by far the largest group of individuals funnel money on up to the next level, which in turn keeps pushing the money higher and higher until it reaches the maybe handful of individuals at the top who are really making all the money. Each "associate" beneath them invests in the "company," which monies simply end up in the grabbing hands of these unsavory types.

By contrast, network marketing is currently one of the fastest growing industries in the country and the world. Though it has existed for decades on end, it is more lucrative now than ever before. These tiered marketing companies exist, ultimately, to sell a product to a consumer. That is why they are real where pyramid schemes are not. They adhere to the laws of supply and demand, where the pyramid scheme-builder is in it to get rich quick off of the efforts and goodwill of countless others. Most importantly, at the end of the day, the pyramid schemer sells *nothing but air*. **Network marketers build a distribution channel.**

THAT IS NOT THE DREAM WE HAVE A MIND TO BUILD

The unscrupulous types we looked at above, those who leave a bad taste in the mouth, could not be more different from you, me and Tranont. Together, we are looking to create lasting change through adding real value to our economies. Our national and individual household economies are inextricably linked and we have to be ready to defend and rebuild both. The effort may seem herculean at times, but starting small leads to big changes. The only wrong choice would be to give up before you even try.

Perhaps you feel oppressed, by your job or by those naysayers we talked about. Well, take heart, as I remember another band of oppressed men and women who rose up against overwhelming opposition to emerge victorious despite the odds against them. I am speaking of the very founding of our nation, the United States of America. Our Founding Fathers distilled the clear essence of an idea called Democracy from the withering husk that was Old Europe. In 1776, our ancestors fought against the tax man, who took from them without giving anything back. King George didn't even grant us the dignity of pretending to consider our views. Well, that fight ended up allowing the dream that was America (and will be once again) to become a reality.

Even when the British came back to burn the White House to the ground in 1814, even as our forefathers stood amidst the stone and splintered wood, ash and smoke rising into the sky, we did not give up. You know what we did? *We built another White House.*

That is the attitude of the America I remember. It can be that way again, all we need to do is revitalize ourselves. By uplifting ourselves, community by community, we will dot the country with enclaves of true freedom, including the financial, spiritual and emotional. Liberty can be metaphorically painted over every doorstep from coast to coast.

We Need a Singular Focus

If the two World Wars taught Germany anything, it is that fighting a battle on two fronts is a surefire way to lose a military campaign. The morale of the story is that, in order to accomplish the renovation of America we dream of, we need to be singular in our focus. We must reach for the starts while maintaining a pragmatic mentality. No easy task lies before us.

Yet, through discipline, you can defeat distraction. Through steadfastness, you can overcome the turmoil and flux of a seemingly random and chaotic world. There is, in fact, order underlying the chaos of the forces at play in this world. A typhoon is effect of a cause, just as every economic boom comes from somewhere. Learning to understand these forces can give you the edge to see patterns where others only pickup clouds of color. That's the gift of Tranont that keeps on giving. The education this company provides you with can help you stay focused on sniffing out the trail to the pile of money when all the other dogs are content themselves with chasing squirrels.

However, it is equally important to remember that, despite needing to be business-minded and practical in your approach of customers and partners alike, your dream is the fuel for your success. Thus, you must not forget to feed it.

As Mark Twain put it, "You can't depend on your eyes when your imagination is out of focus."

Your dream will keep you going, be your light in the darkness, even as all other lights go out. The key is to progress steadily. Only step when you have tested the waters ahead with a stout stick. If you run too far too fast, you may well end up falling into the swamp and, once there, you will be at the mercy of dangers like crocodiles and quicksand. Avoid these entirely by maintaining a much more measured approach. Be singular in your focus.

In the words of Venus Williams, "I don't focus on what I'm up against. I focus on my goals and I try to ignore the rest." Interpreting this statement, I would not say that she advocates putting blinders over your eyes and pretending that the world around you does not exist. Instead, she, like you must, simply tackles one issue at a time. Rather than worry about the Wimbledon crowds, for example, or how incredible hot it was that day, or how tired she'd become, Williams focused her attention squarely on her opponent. That is what made her number one in the world.

GO FORTH WITH CONFIDENCE IN YOURSELF

There is no such thing as failure.
There are only results.

- Tony Robbins

Presentation is critical when putting yourself and your business idea out there. Harvey Mackay, businessman, author and syndicated columnist, says that, "You don't need a big close, as many sales reps believe. You risk losing your customer when you save all the good stuff for the end. Keep the customer actively involved throughout your presentation, and watch your results improve."

Keeping your customers, as well as your future partners, engaged long enough to reach the end of the pitch means having plenty of evidence proving the viability of your idea. By the way, you will never convince anyone if you are not yet convinced yourself. Before moving on to the recruitment phase, you will have to be sure of your own passion. Do you really believe in this undertaking, in its possibilities for success, in its inherent worth?

"Once you make the decision you will find all the people, resources, and ideas you need... Every time."

-Bob Proctor

Luckily, with Tranont on your side, in no time at all you will be educated enough to quell the doubts of even your harshest critics. For one thing, if you are confronted with the accusation that you are pushing a pyramid scheme, you will have the vocabulary to dispel such notions. You may already have had to deal with this sort of issue, but many people will simply be content to define a pyramid scheme in nebulous terms. They will say that, in such a scheme, there are a few people at the top making all the money and many at the bottom making nothing at all. When they ask you how your proposition differs from a pyramid scheme, you can tell them what you will have learned from this chapter and from Tranont. But you can also ask, with just a tinge of playfulness, a question of your questioner: "Is it not true that, where you work, there are a few people at the top (CEOs, partners, presidents, etc.) who make most of the money, while the many at the bottom (associates, cashiers, clerks, etc.) make much less?"

At the very least, your method for making real money is geared toward freeing yourself and your colleagues from this sort of servitude. You have one more advantage, as well. People tend to remember anecdotes or, better yet, personalized stories of triumph much better than they do dryly presented strategies for success. Just as the key players in Tranont have their own unique stories, your partnership with this company primes you to create and present your own wonderful tale. Relate to the person you are addressing, and you will be sure to win them over.

You Will be Faced with Questions

When pitching your idea to potential partners, they may very well come back with prepared questions. Why should they invest? They read this or that online, what do you think of that? The possibilities are endless, which is why you should preempt them. Snatch and hold the initiative by keeping them on the defensive. I do not mean you should assault them verbally or physically or anything similar. No, instead you must mount an offensive by asking your own questions, supported by evidence.

- Here is what I am presenting to you. Knowing that X is true, would you not say Y is true also, given the following reasons?
- And, if so, why would you not invest?
- Considering how lucrative Market A is, I see a real opportunity here to establish ourselves in this niche. Knowing this, would you like to join me?

By continuously asking them questions that cause them to consider what is stopping them, you are more likely to break through even the hardest of shells.

One of these days, though, you will deal with someone whose opinion is truly immutable. No matter what you say, no matter how much supporting evidence you present, this person will not change his or her mind. And, you know what, that is fine. Even if this individual is very close to you, a friend, a sibling or what have you, you should respect his or her right to not enter into business with you.

Building a business requires building strong relationships. In the end, the relationship trumps all. To preserve yours, you will need to know when you are fighting a losing battle and, thus, when to cut your losses. As long as you honestly and openly presented 100 percent of the information you had, you can rest assured that this person has made an informed decision. What's done is done and no harm, no foul.

"That's what wealthy people do. They build their ark way before it rains. And if people don't want to get on the ship, that's okay, they drown. People right now in my life are drowning because they didn't listen… It's not my fault, I tried."

-Jake Spencer

If all of your attempts at persuasion should fail, it is important to accept refusal with dignity. Take that "no" for an answer, in other words, but maybe leave this person with the words of Theodore Roosevelt:

"Far better is it to dare mighty things, to win glorious triumphs, even though checkered by failure... than to rank with those poor spirits who neither enjoy nor suffer much, because they live in a gray twilight that knows not victory nor defeat."

If you can't call that food for thought, what would qualify?

A Dangerous Mistake

Depending to a degree on the business in question, though this principle applies almost universally, it takes all types and stripes to build a business. And, though it is at time unfortunate, you cannot make a tiger change his stripes. Those you think would be perfect partners may end up snubbing you or, if hired on, not quite the right fit. On the other hand, men and women you would think are completely unsuitable could possibly have become incredible assets to you and your company.

> "You don't build a business – you build people – and then people build the business."
>
> -Zig Ziglar

You can't ask a tiger to change his stripes, but it is up to you to interpret the pattern. Just because someone does not dress in Armani suits and wear snake skin boots does not mean this person is bad with money. Spendthrifts and paupers occupy two very distinct categories. Stereotyping is a dangerous folly of a pastime and one that will only harm your recruitment efforts in the long term.

Now that that caveat is out of the way, let's talk about an important planning tool.

THE EVOLVING CONTACT LIST

Before you can reach out to the people in your life with a mutually beneficial offer, you first should create a comprehensive list of all of these individuals and rank them according to specific criteria, such as importance to you and how much influence you have over them.

You might think the list must be limited to family members, friends and colleagues. However, there is no reason why you shouldn't reach out to neighbors, fellow churchgoers, your financial consultant, your cell phone contacts, old high school and college associates, your children's teachers, the parents of your children's friends and many, many more. Think on it for an hour and you are sure to come up with loads of interesting prospects. Anyone you can think of who has a good head on his or her shoulders. In essence, anyone with whom you do some sort of business should be investigated. Will he or she be useful and will he or she benefit?

I call this an "evolving contact list" because you should think of it as a living, breathing thing. As you meet more people, you will add more names to list. As your own contacts add to their lists, you will expand your own.

Consider the pros and cons of each individual on the list. Recruit them based on business acumen, skill sets, assets they can contribute and other criteria. Soon enough, you will have many valuable partners, each with a stake in the wellbeing and advancement of your business. Those who will be successful in your new venture are hiding in plain sight and it is up to you to root them out like Easter Eggs in the backyard.

BEWARE ONE TRICKY NETWORKING TRAP

As you are building this expansive and expanding empire through recruiting partners and associates, you may come across one pitfall that can doom a start business. While it is of course a fine idea to foster a policy of open-mindedness, beware allowing unsavory individuals into the fold.

You will be careful in whom you recruit, assuring yourself of their financial credibility and success-oriented dispositions. Those you take under your wing, however, may refer less stable types to you yourself would. They will do this with the best of intentions, most likely, but the fact remains that the longevity and power of your business depends on the quality of your hires. Therefore, you cannot justify hiring your friend Jeff's poor old Uncle Bill, no matter how charming of a fellow he might prove to be. If he is flat broke, chances are there is a very good reason. Maybe he is simply down on his luck, but the root of the cause may rely on his own conduct and choices to a far greater degree than either he, or those around him (including Jeff), would care to admit.

Consider each applicant on a case by case basis and don't hesitate to turn someone down if he or she should happen to rub you the wrong way. On a closely related note: do not give anyone, even your own siblings, preferential treatment. This will help to ensure that you hire the right individuals right away, saving you time, money, heart- and headaches along the way.

If you can readily vouch for the character of your new hire, however, it is likely that he or she is of sound mind and character and thus you should run into problems less frequently.

Keep a To-Do List

Staying on top of all the obligations of a Twenty-First Century life can feel next to impossible at times. Running a family, taking the kids to school, to band practice, spending time with the in-laws, getting the car tuned up, the tasks pile up endlessly. Add to that the responsibilities pertaining to running a business and it becomes quite easy to see how anyone could quickly become overwhelmed.

Fortunately, there is a solution so elegant but simple that you may feel I have lost my mind for even daring to suggest it. *Writing a daily to-do list*, however, can *change your life*. Does that seem like an exaggeration? I assure you that I am not being hyperbolic.

For one thing, the act of writing things down can make all of those tasks seem much more manageable. Our minds habitually play tricks on us, including the hyperinflation of obligations into a seemingly unmanageable pile. Most of us have probably seen the old cartoons in which a closet is stuffed full of junk to the point where, when someone dares open the door, all of it floods out, usually crushing the opener. Avoid having your mind exhibiting the properties of that cartoon closet door; write a to-do list.

Secondly, I don't know about you, but I can, at times, be a bit forgetful. It happens to the best of us, to be sure, but when you are managing a business, you can't exactly afford to have billing issues or project submission deadlines slip your mind. Putting to paper all of the concerns facing you will put everything in perspective.

While it may seem tempting, it is rarely a good idea to have your to-do lists span a week, a month or more. Looking at everything all at once could discourage you, defeating the purpose of this time- and aggravation-saving tool. Wisdom dictates that you keep your to-do lists focused on *today*. For items whose deadlines are further off, you have a calendar.

Now, when we are talking about a to-do list and "putting things to paper," I am not limiting you to physical ink and paper. We live in a digital age and you may find yourself preferring a to-do list uploaded to your smartphone or tablet, or one that is accessible anywhere thanks to the Cloud. Some of you will still prefer to write things out by hand, as this activity triggers the brain in a different way. Any of these options is absolutely fine. The takeaway is to keep yourself on target, keep that *singular focus* we mentioned in sight, using an organized to-do list.

Don't neglect the prioritization of items according to a number system or some similar approach. Completion of the objective, "call to set up lunch meeting with sponsor" is probably more vital to your operation than "buy more ballpoint pens for office." A to-do list allows you to maintain focus, keep your approach aligned with you goals and to prioritize.

There is no "Silver Bullet"

Starting a business and killing a werewolf have absolutely nothing in common. Included in that long list of dissimilarities is that, while you can put a lycanthrope down with a silver bullet, you will never find a magic fix for any of the tasks running your business requires you to undertake.

From recruiting partners and associates to presenting "the pitch" to prospective buyers, your best weapons are your professionalism and determination. As we discussed above, when convincing someone to join forces with you to your mutual benefit, you must set a time, get in the door and be confident — but you must not be too forceful in how you handle the situation. Your attitude must be inviting and you must approach the prospect with all due humility, and only after you have made them realize you are credible and authoritative can you present an offer of partnership or goods.

There has never been, nor will there ever be, just one person, method or product that will, with any degree of certainty whatsoever, lead to you to the end of the road of immense success. Only through team-wide *concerted effort* will you be able to rise to the top and stay there.

Establishing a team requires getting all of those people, who perhaps come from different walks of life, under the same tent and seeing to it that they each come to share your vision. Convincing some will be easier than others. Family and close friends will likely be more amenable to joining you in realizing your unique selling proposition (USP). Those who need a bit more persuading will attempt to shut you down before you can even get to persuading them. To preempt their preempting, you will have to convince them that it is worth their time to hear you out. Evidence, facts and figures will be most helpful to you in such instances.

DRIVING THE SAME POINT HOME, AGAIN AND AGAIN

As you work to convince others of the validity and viability of your idea — and, believe me, it can feel like *work* — you should remind yourself that changing people's minds can take many, many reiterations of the same point on your part.

There is a theory in marketing called "effective frequency," which, in the simplest terms, has to do with the number of times an individual must be exposed, on average, to a particular ad campaign before the point of conversion is reached and the sale is made. That same basic principle applies perfectly to this situation. You may have to present your ideas multiple times before you break past the barriers a given individual has set up.

Without coming across an incredible, overbearing irritant, you will need to be thorough in your presentations and, to some extent, forceful. However, you can more ably overcome this problem by employing a varied approach. Just as an ad campaign (an effective one anyway) would not send out the same ad over and over, you cannot expect your information to strike someone differently the second, third or twelfth time if it still looks and sounds exactly the same. Therefore, you must vary the metaphorical packaging of your presentation.

But, I understand, this is easy enough to say when only keeping to abstract statements. Here is an actual example of this sort of process, one which, depending on the situation and with some variation, could apply to either a sales or recruitment pitch:

1. A Google search lands the prospect on your website's page, where he or she finds access to all sorts of helpful information
2. The user applies for your newsletter, eBook, mail-order DVDs and any other materials you may offer
3. The next step is signing this person up for webinars, or conducting a phone/Skype conference
4. Then, for recruitment purposes, you will meet in your office or at home, depending on the level of familiarity hitherto established
5. Finally, in line with Step 4, set up a corporate meeting with the team at, for instance, a hotel event

At each stage, you will present yourself, your team and what your company stands for in a new light. By the end of it, you should have won over a valuable asset to furthering your plans.

WHAT SEPARATES YOU FROM THE PACK

In a nutshell, what distinguishes you from so many start-ups all across this country is the service-oriented work ethic you share with Tranont. This disposition, if properly managed over time, can easily place you on a pedestal above your competition.

Once your *residual income* machine is pumping out capital at high speed, not only will you be able to invest in yourself and your family, but you will be bettering your neighborhood, subdivision, town, city, county, state and country. With Tranont's framework to support you in your endeavors, spreading the good word has never been easier. And you stand to make a lot of money doing exactly that.

THE DREAM

Distilled down to its essence, the dream you are fighting for, that New American Dream, is to create a company which does not need you. More accurately, you seek to build an operation that is so streamlined, powerful and effective that it generates passive, *residual* income for you every month with minimal to no oversight needed from you. Will you have to work hard to get to that point? Almost certainly. Will the ends justify the means? Indubitably.

To accomplish this laudable feat, you will need to create a company culture that is the envy of all of your competitors. You will need to encourage a culture whose aspects include:

- Standardization

Your materials, including the website, DVDs, YouTube videos and so on, should be unified in the message they put out there for the entire Internet world to see. Standardization also helps your team stay on point. Skype videoconferences and other modern tools can be of great use in creating and preserving unity.

- Expertise

In the same vein as the point above, you should regularly schedule and host training events to ensure that your team is up to snuff and ready to meet any challenge. Make them experts, one and all, in the subject matter pertinent to your operations and goals. A note on hosting events: make sure that the way in which you host a meeting at your home, for example, is simple to *duplicate*. Following the same logic that dictates that you would not want to present conflicting messages to a client, you would not want to make that mistake with your employees. After all, if they are going to go out there and spread the word about your business and Tranont, you will want them to do it in the way you deem best. In short, do not present a "do as I say, not as I do" way of doing things. You will more easily build alliances if you maintain an even hand.

- Authoritativeness

When approaching prospects, your team should be able to rely on your authority. You hold the "upline" position, you are the leader. Don't be afraid to encourage your employees to rely on their immediate superiors, either. Closing a sale can be made much easier with a strong, unified organization at your back. These same rules apply to you, too, should you happen to have a boss, which could very well be the case if, say, someone recruited you into Tranont. Remember that, whoever you decide should make the call or meet with the client, your chosen representative should be someone whose personality matches up with that of the prospect's to the fullest extent possible. For example, an accountant on staff should deal with clients who have a strong background in finance. Someone on your team who happens to be a mom could perhaps relate better to a fellow mother.

- Competitiveness

We would not want anyone to become petty, but there is nothing wrong with a little bit of healthy competition among the ranks. Such motivation can lead your team to seriously increase its potential. You can incentivize a spot of competitive behavior by offering rewards for meeting certain objectives. Whoever is fastest, most effective, receives the greatest number of five-star ratings, whatever the metric you choose, you will find that the drive to excel and emerge victorious very often outweighs the craving for money. When allocating rewards or conducting a performance review, however, always be sure to frame your comments in terms of which of your associates *grew the most.* That way, there are winners, but no real losers, only those who could do better next time. Most importantly, make a point to recognize the efforts of each of your team members. Acknowledge their triumphs as quickly as you would their foibles or mistakes. That also happens to be the Tranont way.

Creating a company which embodies these cultures will ensure that your efforts are streamlined, sensible and efficient. Furthermore, any *secondary recruiting* (when your associates recruit for you) initiatives will be that much more effective.

TRANSFORMING ASSOCIATES INTO LEADERS

Bringing about the New American Dream will only be possible through the consistent and constant transformation of job-stuck individuals into free leaders. The business model of Tranont makes this possible, but it can only be done through your involvement and through the efforts of your associates.

Over the course of your construction of a residual income machine, you will be adding value to the American economy by transforming your associates into true leaders. Everyone has that potential in them. We were all born with it. But your service to the country will be bringing that admirable quality in people to the forefront, all while enriching yourself and your family, of course.

To help you along in the process of generating heroes in your business, here are several qualities typically found in leaders:

- Strong work ethic and desire to succeed
- Integrity; they lead by example and hold the right party/parties responsible (including themselves)
- Influence, in part born of being a true "people person"
- Attractiveness to other leaders
- Internally motivated
- Motivational: they believe in others and bring out the best in them
- Competitive
- Snappy dressers, they take pride in maintaining a professional appearance
- Pragmatism; a true leader will not need to over-complicate the issue by changing things up just for the sake of change; "if it ain't broke, don't fix it"
- Indefatigable spirit; a leader does not lie, cheat or surrender

Find associates with such qualities, and there is no limit to what you will be able to achieve.

Now that we have covered *residual income*, creating a business and issues related to these points, let's move on to how Tranont can deliver very tantalizing results and enable you to build *real wealth*.

The Seven Different Ways to Earn

At long last, we have arrived at the point in this book in which we can specifically discuss the seven different ways you can earn residual income through Tranont all while enriching those around you. We will be covering them, in order, in the upcoming sections. For the sake of convenience, however, here they are in a list:

1. Monthly Team Bonus
2. JeepTM Bonus
3. Life Bonus
4. Builder, Management and Executive Bonus Pools
5. Tranont Life Commissions
6. Promotional Trips and Incentives
7. Retail Preferred Customer Acquisition Bonus

Please be mindful of the fact that the following types of compensation may since have been enhanced by Tranont in an effort to increase the earning potential of its associates. At the time of writing, however, they operated as described below.

Now, without further ado, let's move on through these, one by one, shall we?

MONTHLY TEAM BONUS

As soon as you personally sponsor three active associates, recruiting them into the Tranont fold, you qualify for this bonus. Tranont calls this the "Get 3 — Get Your Product Free" step. This bonus puts a $100 monthly bonus in your account just for keeping three active associates on staff. $100, by the way, happens to be the cost of the monthly utility for joining Tranont and using its multitudes of services. Meaning your membership will be, for all intents and purposes, free, just as long as you meet this minimal requirement. In addition, the amount of this bonus will increase as your number of associates does. Tranont call this GV (or, "group volume") and all you need to know is that "the more the merrier" is your rule of thumb, here.

JEEP™ BONUS

This bonus is yours as soon as you attain the rank of Financial Consultant with Tranont, accomplished by recruiting more associates into your organization. Once done, you will actually receive a $500 monthly payment toward the purchase of an approved Jeep™. Tranont calls this its "Drive to FC" program ("FC" standing for "Financial Consultant").

LIFE BONUS

Senior Financial Consultants receive contributions toward their Tranont Life insurance policies (new or previously existing), courtesy of Tranont. With each increase in rank, Tranont will upgrade its contributions to said policy. Because of this benefit, you can rest assured that the wellbeing of your loved ones will be looked after even should tragedy strike. Not to mention that you will be saving money on those premiums.

BONUS POOLS

In addition to the above-mentioned bonuses, three other types of bonuses apply to Tranont associates who participate in the pool by personally sponsoring new associates. Each member earns a share of a 2 percent bonus pool for every six new associates brought on by him or her.

Once an associate reaches Senior Financial Consultant rank, his or her take comes from the Management Bonus Pool. Each Senior Financial Consultant receives up to five shares of a 4 percent pool.

Those who reach the rank of Vice President draw from the Executive Pool which grants up to four shares of a 9 percent cut.

Tranont Life Commissions

Tranont Life licensed professionals gain access to a powerful suite of products designed to bring about Tranont's vision for a revitalized America by helping you achieve your financial goals, including the acquisition of excellent and affordable insurance. In the process of promoting and selling Tranont Life's great products, you will earn income through a very attractive and, therefore, competitive compensation and promotion program. As you climb the ranks in Tranont Life, your earned income will only increase, thus building real and lasting wealth.

Promotional Trips and Other Incentives

As if the previously described perks were not enough, Tranont also offers access to regular promotion and incentive programs in order to encourage its associates (you and your team) to build upon their existing interpersonal, professional relationships. Fostering this tight-knit attitude leads to a brighter financial future for all involved.

Retail Preferred Customer Acquisition Bonus

Though it is hard to believe, there may be some people out there who, when presented with the opportunity to join Tranont in its endeavors, will turn you down. We discussed the need to accept "no" for an answer and Tranont is definitely on the same page. Those who would rather not become full associates but still wish to make use of some of Tranont's amazing products and services are styled "Preferred

196 | David Adlard   —   American Dream Again

Customers." If you sponsor such a person, as a commission, you will receive 10 percent of his or her monthly subscription. Finally, if you happen to have a sponsor yourself, he or she will receive a 5 percent commission on that same subscription. Thus, it is quite obvious that, if you happen to be the boss or furthest upline in your organization, the more associates you bring, the more money you will make.

Now That the Details Are Out of the Way

I want to reinforce how invaluable Tranont is to the vision so many of us have for an America reborn, an America in which people like you can achieve their wildest dreams through determination and can-do spirit. Thank you for persevering to this point. You are proof that my opinion has value, that it is valid. By virtue of arriving at the end of this chapter, you have demonstrated a fortitude and endurance that you will take with you into your every venture.

There really is nothing stopping you. If nothing else, I hope this chapter, as well as the ones preceding it, have shown you that much.

Tranont Works for You

With such a powerful ally to lean on, building up a business and creating your own version of the New American Dream is more achievable now than ever before. Join forces with Tranont and you will find doors opening into vast new treasure troves you never even knew existed.

The final chapter will summarize the points covered, after which sections we will talk about what comes next. What's the next step? How will you begin your grand journey? Let's keep going. We are so close, now.

8.

THE NEXT STEP

Pat yourself on the back, you've earned it! You have made it to the end of this book, which means you are just about ready to start your journey toward true financial freedom. That New American Dream is so close now that you can practically hear it calling out to you.

Two final tasks lie before us, to be completed in this chapter. First, we will go over a summary of the major points covered in this book. Then, we will talk about where to go from here. Alright, let's get to it.

SUMMARY OF POINTS

1. That Picket Fence Could Use a Fresh Coat: The Millennial Herd and the Death of the Old American Dream

In Chapter 1, we introduced what I call the Old American Dream, that outdated notion that anyone can get good grades, earn a degree, get a good job, work about three or four decades and retire to relative comfort. We were all told to buy a home, maybe put up a white picket fence and sit there, awaiting something better, something for which we had no name. It was never properly described to us, this Old American Dream. We thought it was the only way. Therefore, when it was revealed to be untenable in today's world, most of us either didn't know how to effectively respond, or ignored the truth entirely.

We saw the facts and figures revealing the fundamental death of that Old American Dream, yet we also saw how the government and various institutions still profit from this dream-turned-myth. That is why it prevails, even today, despite its destruction. So many of us live in the dark, despite the truth being so readily apparent. All it requires is that we pay attention, and we can see the student loan crisis, rampant credit card debt, loss of any social safety nets, lifestyle standards plummeting and many other troubling factors of modern life for exactly what they are: harbingers of change. The tide has shifted, and the wise will adapt.

You don't want to have to work longer, harder and faster, maybe into your seventies, maybe beyond. You don't want to pay into social security with no guarantees that you will ever see any of that money put to use protecting you and your family (in fact, it's likely social security will be utterly annihilated within several years to a few decades). You don't want to be stuck in debt, paying off a second mortgage, all those credit cards and that car that isn't quite so new anymore.

2. The New American Dream

Chapter 2 presented an answer to the above-stated fears by describing a better, newer dream fit for the modern world. I call this one the New American Dream. What is it? The story of the American spirit, of entrepreneurship, of *starting your own business.*

We pulled statistics that showed us how a huge percentage of the nation's (and world's) top earners are, in fact, small business owners. Working for someone else, you are merely funneling all of your blood, sweat and tears into making his or her dream into a reality. Is that really what you want?

Of course not! And that is why we looked some concepts set forth by Robert Kiyosaki in his books *Rich Dad Poor Dad and The CashFlow Quadrant Guide to Financial Freedom.* His work showed us how to start thinking about transforming ourselves from worker bees into squad commanders and, finally, the queen bee, herself. By becoming a business owner and investing, you can build your asset column while shrinking your liabilities.

Remember — this one throws a lot of people off — that your car and home are not assets. They are liabilities. They cost you money. Only those investments of yours that generate income can be considered true assets.

3. Tranont: A Company Dedicated to Helping Americans

This chapter introduced you to Tranont and its suite of products designed to save you money and educate you about the intricacies of the financial industry. We saw how, thanks to the unique philosophy of Tranont, bolstered by amazing services, anyone could build real wealth and achieve the New American Dream — provided he or she is motivated, of course.

We also discussed Kathleen Rich-New's work, *Plan B: The Real Deal Guide to Creating Your Business,* which told us the importance of using one's Plan A to fund an exciting Plan B. In essence, stick with the day job and build your business part-time, channeling ever greater amounts of effort and money into the latter, as time goes on. In Chapter 3, we also covered the various types of businesses you might start, as well as the requirements (financial and otherwise) demanded of each one.

These concepts, combined with the amazing business opportunity Tranont offers, really started to reveal tremendous opportunities for growth. With Tranont you, too, can *Change Life Rapidly!*

4. The Products to Shape the Future

Here we discovered the excellent products and services offered by Tranont, each designed to help Americans cope with an area of difficulty in starting or managing their own businesses. Whether you need to brush up on your skill set, increase your financial literacy, learn about the incredibly complex tax codes, protect your and your company's online identities or complete any one of an expansive number of tasks including, Tranont has the answers to your questions and concerns.

The core products included Tranont OneView, Tranont Defend, Tranont Tax and Tranont Education, respectively dealing with financial overviews, online security, taxes and financial literacy.

Credit card processing, background checks, VOIP business phone services and many more products provide comprehensive and very effective business to business communication solutions. Add to these cell phone service partnerships with Verizon and, soon, AT&T and T-Mobile, and you have yourself an industry leader, no two ways about it.

The company's licensed products include the fabulous Tranont Life, LLC. With insurance and investment products that can quickly grant a very attractive additional revenue stream to its partners and associates, Tranont quickly established itself as the best option for new business owners. You learned how to really get off on the right foot by earning *residual income,* all while partnering with a constantly expanding, high-powered, industry-leading company.

5. The Rising Stars and Key Players of Tranont

Rather than simply taking my word for it, you investigated the real-life success stories of American business owners. Thanks to Tranont, these individuals turned their lives around and renewed their prospects, some becoming wealthier than they ever could have dreamed.

6. Be Your Own Bank

In this chapter, we talked about the Private/Smart Banking Concept, recommending books for further reading. Investing in life insurance quickly revealed itself to the keystone of the bridge to true financial freedom. By becoming your own bank, you could pay yourself interest that would otherwise go to credit card companies, banks and other institutions. While protecting your family with amazing benefits, you could build real wealth, accessing your liquid cash anytime you needed and never again losing money unnecessarily to interest payments and other drains on your portfolio. Through Tranont Life's proprietary Index Universal Life program, you could generate astounding returns unmatched by any other company.

7. The Opportunity

Finally, in Chapter 7, you were introduced to the seven different ways to earn residual income. Learning about all the tools presented in this book, you were shown how to claim your New American Dream and hold onto it forever.

In addition, you saw just how different Tranont is from any other company, even those also considered to be "multi-level marketing" firms. The tiers of bonuses, the first few of which are *especially* rapidly achievable, are absurdly attractive. Earn *residual income,* the path to lasting wealth, just for spreading the good word about Tranont to family, friends, coworkers, acquaintances and so on. You could even get a Jeep paid for by the company, if you work your way up the ranks.

Which brings us back to this current chapter, our summary completed. You now have the tools at your disposal to begin your journey to success, but one question remains.

What's the Next Step?

There's a mantra I like to keep close to my heart:

"If you keep doing what you've been doing, then things aren't going to change."

What statement could be simpler or easier to understand? Despite how obvious this logical thought might be, so few folks actually internalize it. Fewer still actually put it to practice.

What aspects of your life would *you* want to change? For just one minute, forget about your boss, your friends, even your spouse. Just think about *you*. What do you want to see rapidly change in your day-to-day?

"If you change the way you look at things, the things you look at change."

-Wayne Dyer

Tranont can give you the keys to the vehicle that will drive you into the brightest future you can imagine, maybe even brighter. But don't just take my word for it. This is your life we are talking about. It's up to you to make this critical decision.

I would like to make one suggestion, if I may. One of our Founding Fathers, the great Benjamin Franklin, came up with a great way to weigh the merits of various options against each other in order to choose the best of the bunch.

Benjamin Franklin's Method

Old Ben, the scientist, diplomat, scholar and gentleman that he was, had an extraordinarily reasonable approach to the decision making process. When asked for advice by friends, he would often tell them he couldn't, in good conscience, tell them what to do without knowing all the facts. Therefore, he would explain how he decided on a course of action, so that they could emulate him.

You are probably quite familiar with the technique. Benjamin Franklin extolled the virtues of creating a list of *pros and cons*. Where he differs from many modern, hurried Americans, however, is in his patience. He would think about the issue at hand for *days* on end. In fact, he recommended one take three or four days to come to a conclusion.

Regardless of the amount of time you devote to this pursuit, the technique itself is exceedingly simple.

1. Divide a sheet of paper in half with a line
2. Create headers on either side of the divide, one entitled "Pro," the other "Con"
3. Spend the time really digging for Pros and Cons to add to the list
4. If after some time (Franklin recommended one to two days) no more additions present themselves, you can move on to the next step
5. Weigh the pros against the cons, striking those that are equal. Remember, the ratio doesn't need to be one-to-one; three cons could be worth four pros, in which case you would cross out a total of seven items
6. Once done with step 5, you just have to count the pros and the cons
7. If the pros outweigh the cons, you can confidently proceed knowing that you thought your course of action through, eliminating all of the reasons why you might feel uneasy

And that's all there is to it.

Take a sheet of paper and devote some time to thinking about Tranont. However, I, for one, feel that you will soon see that the pros greatly outweigh the paltry few cons (if there even are any!). Consider your situation, all the strife and turmoil in your life, and decide from there.

To get you started, here are a few pros covered in this book. Tranont gives you, among other benefits:

- The tools to build your very own business
- The ability to free yourself from your dead-end or overly stressful job

- Financial education courses that will turn you into a highly literate finance guru, if you choose to become one
- Bonuses galore, including payments toward a Jeep and, most importantly, *residual income*
- Freedom from debt and the constant worry over money
- Peace of mind, knowing that you and your family will finally be able to comfortably live the life you have always dreamed of

TRANONT IS WAITING FOR YOU

The only thing standing between you and the achievement of real wealth is hesitancy. I understand that the prospect of change can seem frightening, at first. After all, you have been leading the same kind of life for years and years, maybe even decades, by now. How could you hope to climb out of the debt abyss into which you were flung right out of college? How could you hope to ever pay off that house? How could you expect to change your situation?

Well, maybe you could do it alone. Maybe through some extraordinary, super-human exertion of will you could singlehandedly dig yourself up from the seemingly infinitely expanding ditch of debt. But, I ask you, *why would you want to?*

Why would you want to go for it alone? There is help out there. You have your pride, just as I do, just as so many Americans do. Still, keeping yourself in the dark and the cold for the sake of that pride is not the right thing to do. That is not justice, but injustice. You have to remember you deserve better. You deserve that New American Dream we have been talking about. And, you know what, your children deserve it, too. They ought to inherit what Mom and Dad worked so hard to build. Do you want what little you manage to scrimp and save to be snatched up by the government once you're gone? Should the tax man be entitled to your children's inheritance?

The answer to that question should be a resounding "no." Now, let me ask you this: do you want the power to pull yourself up by your own bootstraps? Of course you do, because that's the American way. That supreme can-do spirit is what made this country great in the first place.

You have done everything right. You ought to get your long-deserved reward for all those years of hard work.

Tranont can help.

The company cannot do everything for you, but you wouldn't want it that way, anyway. You are a go-getter, as they say. You keep pushing for a better future. What Tranont does is give you the tools to do what you do already in a better, more effective way. Tranont has a suite of products that can help you start your very own business as well as put it on the map.

Isn't it time you started working *towards* something, rather than *for* someone else? Tranont can see to it that you get in gear and progress toward the future you have always wanted.

Reach Out

Reaching out to claim your dream can become part of your daily existence. Wake up in the morning, make yourself breakfast, go to work and then *build your business.* Committing on a daily basis to your future success will allow you to eventually pour an ever-increasing portion of your energies into your own projects, your own aspirations and objectives.

Tranont offers the technologies, resources and professional advice to help you meet all of your professional goals. Transform yourself. Change your life rapidly.

All you need to do to get started is reach out to the person who gave you this book. Whoever first clued you in to the existence of this amazing company can no doubt fully bring you into the fold.

I am not ashamed to admit that I am very excited for you, and more than a little envious of your position: you have a thrilling time ahead of you. Starting a business is one of the greatest, most liberating experiences this wonderful country has to offer. It has made my left very worthwhile.

Thank you so much for choosing to take the first steps of your journey with me. I am honored that you did.

David Adlard

Made in the USA
San Bernardino, CA
11 November 2015